CW00404149

# MEDIEVAL
## TOWNS

## Social History in Perspective

General Editor: Jeremy Black

*Social History in Perspective* is a series of in-depth studies of the
many topics in social, cultural and religious history.

### PUBLISHED

John Belchem *Popular Radicalism in Nineteenth-Century Britain*
Sue Bruley *Women in Britain Since 1900*
Simon Dentith *Society and Cultural Forms in Nineteenth-Century England*
Joyce M. Ellis *The Georgian Town, 1680–1840*
Peter Fleming *Family and Household in Medieval England*
Kathryn Gleadle *British Women in the Nineteenth Century*
Harry Goulbourne *Race Relations in Britain since 1945*
Anne Hardy *Health and Medicine in Britain since 1860*
Tim Hitchcock *English Sexualities, 1700–1800*
Sybil M. Jack *Towns in Tudor and Stuart Britain*
Helen M. Jewell *Education in Early Modern England*
Alan Kidd *State, Society and the Poor in Nineteenth-Century England*
Arthur J. McIvor *A History of Work in Britain, 1880–1950*
Hugh McLeod *Religion and Society in England, 1850–1914*
Donald M. MacRaild *Irish Migrants in Modern Britain, 1750–1922*
Donald M. MacRaild and David E. Martin *Labour in Britain, 1830–1914*
Christopher Marsh *Popular Religion in the Sixteenth Century*
Michael A. Mullett *Catholics in Britain and Ireland, 1558–1829*
R.Malcolm Smuts *Culture and Power in England, 1585–1685*
John Spurr *English Puritanism, 1603–1689*
W.B. Stephens *Education in Britain, 1750–1914*
Heather Swanson *Medieval British Towns*
David Taylor *Crime, Policing and Punishment in England, 1750–1914*
N.L. Tranter *British Population in the Twentieth Century*
Ian D. Whyte *Migration and Society in Britain, 1550–1830*
Ian D. Whyte *Scotland's Society and Economy in Transition, c.1500–c.1760*

Please note that a sister series, *British History in Perspective*, is available,

---

### Social History in Perspective
### Series Standing Order
ISBN 0–333–71694–9 hardcover
ISBN 0–333–69336–1 paperback
*(outside North America only)*

You can receive future titles in this series as they are published by placing a standing order.
Please contact your bookseller or, in case of difficulty, write to us at the address below with
your name and address, the title of the series and the ISBN quoted above.

Customer Services Department, Macmillan Distribution Ltd
Houndmills, Basingstoke, Hampshire RG21 6XS, England

# MEDIEVAL BRITISH TOWNS

Heather Swanson
*Associate Lecturer,*
*the Open University*

palgrave

© Heather Swanson 1999

All rights reserved. No reproduction, copy or transmission of this publication may be made without written permission.

No paragraph of this publication may be reproduced, copied or transmitted save with written permission or in accordance with the provisions of the Copyright, Designs and Patents Act 1988, or under the terms of any licence permitting limited copying issued by the Copyright Licensing Agency, 90 Tottenham Court Road, London W1P 0LP.

Any person who does any unauthorised act in relation to this publication may be liable to criminal prosecution and civil claims for damages.

The author has asserted her right to be identified as the author of this work in accordance with the Copyright, Designs and Patents Act 1988.

Published by
PALGRAVE
Houndmills, Basingstoke, Hampshire RG21 6XS and
175 Fifth Avenue, New York, N.Y. 10010
Companies and representatives throughout the world

PALGRAVE is the new global academic imprint of
St. Martin's Press LLC Scholarly and Reference Division and
Palgrave Publishers Ltd (formerly Macmillan Press Ltd).

*Outside North America*
ISBN 0–333–63360–1 hardcover
ISBN 0–333–63361–X paperback

*Inside North America*
ISBN 0–312–22326–9

This book is printed on paper suitable for recycling and made from fully managed and sustained forest sources.

A catalogue record for this book is available from the British Library.

Library of Congress Cataloging-in-Publication Data
Swanson, Heather.
Medieval British towns / Heather Swanson.
    p. cm— (Social history in perspective)
    Includes bibliographical references and index.
    ISBN 0–312–22326–9 (cloth)
    1. Cities and towns—Great Britain—History. 2. Urbanization–
-Great Britain—History. I. Title. II. Series.
HT133.S934  1999
307.76'0942'0902—dc21                                              99–12187
                                                                                          CIP

10   9   8   7   6   5   4   3   2
09  08  07  06  05  04  03  02

Printed and bound in Great Britain by
Antony Rowe Ltd, Chippenham, Wiltshire

# CONTENTS

Map of towns mentioned in the text

**Key**

| | |
|---|---|
| B | Buntingford |
| C | Cambridge |
| H | Hadleigh |
| Ha | Halesowen |
| L | Lavenham |
| N | Northampton |
| S | Standon |
| SA | Stratford-upon-Avon |
| SS | Shipston on Stour |
| St I | St Ives |
| T | Tewkesbury |

# INTRODUCTION

It was the opinion of Archbishop Pecham in the late thirteenth century that the native Welsh could only be civilised by introducing them to towns planted in the process of English colonisation. His attitude opens up a whole range of questions about the function of British medieval towns – not least because, after the Welsh revolt against the English in 1295, those specifically excluded from being burgesses in Welsh towns were the Welsh, so that the civilising process was likely to be somewhat protracted. Pecham's conception of a town was of a place for the inculcation of manners and learning and the right practice of Christianity. But for Pecham, Christianity on its own was not enough to render the barbarians civilised; only a town constructed in the light of classical values could do that. Was Pecham's vision of the town as the standard-bearer of Roman values, the mirror of classical cities, one that was shared by migrants to towns and the lords who either founded or endeavoured to control them? The answer has to be very probably not. The classical conception of a city does not readily translate into the settlements of $c$.500–1000 people that made up the majority of towns in the British Isles. The small size of these settlements is significant. This book starts from the now generally accepted premise that British towns can be best defined in economic terms: they were places with a concentration of population, however small that population might be, where the majority were engaged in a diversity of non-agricultural occupations.

There were very few towns with populations of over 5000 in the British Isles. In a European context this can make British urbanisation seem insignificant. In his survey of European urban populations, Bairoch calculated that only 5 per cent of British people lived in towns of over 5000 in 1300; in contrast, he estimated that in most of Europe the figure was 10 per cent and in the most densely urbanised areas, the Low Countries and North Italy, 20 per cent.[1] But accepting small towns as genuinely urban does put the whole issue of urbanisation in a new perspective and

1

is indicative of the radical rethinking currently going on about the role of the town in the economy. Towns are being studied in the context of the commercialisation of society as a whole, a commercialisation that took in the whole gamut of money-based transactions, from the petty commodity production of peasants through to international trade and finance.[2] It was a change in which small towns were every bit as significant as the more glamorous international emporia and manufacturing giants, for it was the myriad of local transactions which provided the essential foundation for the entire urban hierarchy. The necessity of focusing on the small towns of Britain because they were so numerous, rather than marking Britain out as unique, may on the contrary draw more attention to the possibility of useful parallels with the role of small towns in other parts of Europe.[3]

Although most British towns were very small, they were still distinct from rural society. Despite the ownership of common fields by urban communities, the agrarian interests of some townspeople, the pigs and the chickens in the street, the town was clearly distinguished from the countryside by its social structure. Thornbury in Gloucestershire is the now classic example of the small town of around 500 inhabitants with some thirty-five separate occupations; it is an example that could be replicated in other parts of the British Isles.[4] To a large extent this specialised economic role was recognised at some point in the town's history by urban privileges, the granting of different legal status to the town, constituting it as a borough. But legal status was not the defining character of a town. In all parts of the British Isles there were places called boroughs that never developed into towns. Equally there were settlements functioning as towns for decades before they were formally made boroughs. What made or broke an urban settlement was the effectiveness of its market. Barrow's judgement on Scottish towns that 'markets could exist without burghs, but a burgh without a market is almost a contradiction in terms' is applicable to all parts of the British Isles.[5] It is a definition that holds good even though the towns in question emerged at different times and under different circumstances. The way in which the urban market functioned is therefore central to this book. After a chronological account of the foundation and growth of towns in Chapter 1, Chapter 2 discusses the urban economy: the extent to which marketing was concentrated in towns; the relationship of rural to urban markets and of small town markets to regional centres; the changing demand for goods and the sources from which these goods were derived – locally, regionally or from overseas.

However, urban markets cannot be studied independently of the political and social structure in which they operated. The idea that the town can be defined as a legally distinct entity is nowadays given short shrift, but it is not something that can be ignored completely, because it mattered to contemporaries. Borough status was seen to confer certain desirable privileges, and within the borough townsmen aspired to self-regulation to defend these. So Chapter 3 looks at the extent to which townspeople were able to participate in the government of their community or to regulate its economy. However, the fact that boroughs were legally distinct and acquired powers of self-government does not mean that they were anomalies in feudal society. Urban historians have now moved a long way from Postan's famous definition of towns as 'non-feudal islands in a feudal sea'.[6] On the contrary, towns are now seen as one expression of feudal lordship, whether that lord be a lay or ecclesiastical magnate or the king himself. It is this perception of the town as an integral part of the structure of power that gives the chronological starting point of this book. The spread of town foundation across the British Isles in the twelfth century served the purposes of Anglo-Norman lords.

The study of medieval British towns concludes in the early sixteenth century. The rationale for this is partly economic; by the 1520s and 1530s there was at last some evidence of sustained population growth, after nearly 170 years of decline or stagnation since the Black Death; with it came some improvement in the economy after the difficult fifteenth century. Chapter 4 looks at what economic change over the whole period from the twelfth to the early sixteenth centuries meant for the wealth and prospects of townsmen and women. But there is another more compelling reason for drawing this study to a close in the early sixteenth century, the onset of religious change. The move to Protestantism was far from uniform across the British Isles. Changes were implemented far earlier in England than in Scotland; in contrast, in Irish towns Protestant evangelism hardly made any impact at all. But the assault on Catholicism throws into relief the fundamental way in which the Catholic Church had articulated medieval urban society. Chapter 4 therefore also considers the ceremony, ritual and forms of social organisation orchestrated by the Church which had expressed urban social structure and urban identity. As the Protestant Reformation stripped these things away, towns had to find a new symbolic vocabulary through which they could be represented, both to themselves and to the world.

So the organisation of the book is mainly thematic, taking in turn the economy, the legal structure and the social organisation of medieval towns. However, given the time-scale involved, it would be very easy to lose sight of any change over time if some chronological framework were not provided. Hence Chapter 1 deals with the process of urbanisation over the twelfth to sixteenth centuries, against which to set the developments outlined in Chapters 2, 3 and 4.

Nowadays the urban historian has to be a resolute and ambitious reader. Basic sources are of course long familiar: civic records; the taxation and judicial records of central government; records of ecclesiastical courts. But as well as using these in studying the fortunes of individual towns, it is necessary to relate towns to each other. In particular, this means looking at the records of the manorial courts that regulated the existence of those towns that never gained the status of borough. Further than this, given that urbanisation was part of a wider commercialisation of society, the urban historian needs to understand change in the rural economy. Mercifully for most of us, the trail has been blazed by the work of a number of historians who have set out methodologies for integrating these different areas of research. Particularly useful in this respect are the works of Mark Bailey, Richard Britnell, Chris Dyer, Rodney Hilton and Maryanne Kowaleski cited in the bibliography.

A particular difficulty for the comparative historian lies in the fact that most of the documentary evidence for medieval towns comes from England. This is true even in the fifteenth century, when documentation from other parts of the British Isles becomes a little less sparse. Hence urban history is in places very dependent on archaeology and town-plan analysis to supplement the absence of written records. The application of theoretical models from other disciplines is also proving very fruitful in understanding the way that the medieval town worked. I have found particularly useful the central place theories of urban geographers (Chapter 2), Rigby's use of the sociological theory of closure (Chapter 3) and gender historians' insights into the nature of patriarchy (Chapter 4).[7] I have included fairly detailed notes with the text in order to give the necessary access to the different debates introduced and the different methodologies used. Not all these works are cited in the Bibliography, which has been kept concise in order that it does not become impenetrable.

It is evident that a book like this is almost wholly dependent on the work of others, and I am acutely aware of the generalisations that have had to be made to the detriment of the subtleties of argument presented by scholars in the field. I am grateful for all the help I have received and would like to thank Steve Bassett for his advice on Anglo-Saxon towns and Pat Dennison for making work in progress from the Scottish Burgh Survey available to me. I owe a particular debt to Chris Dyer, whose insights into the subject have been invaluable in shaping my ideas. Finally, and above all, I want to thank my husband Robert, both for his unending moral support and for his encyclopaedic knowledge of ecclesiastical history, both of which provided an essential foundation for this work.

# 1

## URBANISATION

In order for towns to come into being and to grow, a number of factors needed to converge, and isolating any one of them as the key variable can be a bit misleading. There needed to be economic growth on a scale that would support an urban structure, but the impetus towards town creation and the shape that the urban network took was determined also by the actions of those in power. There are, then, elements of both a bottom-up and a top-down explanation for the emergence of towns in medieval Britain, deriving on the one hand from organic growth, the expansion of the population and the growth of the market, and on the other from the way in which economic growth was stimulated by and manipulated by lords.

Both these elements can be seen operating in Anglo-Saxon England, tentatively from the seventh, more definitely from the eighth century onwards. Towns had decayed in Britain with the collapse of Roman culture, and had disappeared by the sixth century. The substantial ruins of Roman settlements were merely ghosts of urbanisation; the small communities that used their walls for shelter or as a cloak of status were not occupied in trade and industry. Making any statements about when and why Anglo-Saxon towns emerged is to wade into a sea of controversy, much of it the result of different definitions of what constitutes a town. But good candidates as early urban communities are the settlements known as wics, for example Hamwic (subsequently Southampton), Ipswich and Eforwic (subsequently York). Wics were located either on the coast or on the banks of rivers, not just in England, but all round the littoral of the North Sea in the eighth century, constituting an extensive trading community. Where, as at Hamwic and Ipswich, there have been extensive excavations, these places have proved to be substantial settlements, not

6

only for long-distance trade, but also for local trade and for manufacture, making them more than just centres for the exchange of luxuries. Some wics were abandoned by the ninth century and some of them appear to have moved site: the settled areas at Hamwic, York and London migrated some way along their respective river banks. Nonetheless significant wics marked points of exchange that had subsequent continuous histories as towns.

Hamwic and Ipswich appear to have been founded on greenfield sites, not near any previous significant settlement. However, some wics were located near to important foci of political and ecclesiastical power, as at York and London. But taking the town as defined by its occupational heterogeneity, in these instances it was essentially the commercial settlement which endowed the site with its urban character. For places of religious significance and places of political importance cannot be assumed automatically to have generated towns. Large institutions may have accumulated small settlements around them, but, for example at Canterbury, a major ecclesiastical centre, there is minimal evidence of commerce in the seventh century; its *raison d'être* was religious and administrative and it was not performing the functions of a town.[1] Places like seventh-century Canterbury are best referred to as pre-urban nuclei or proto-towns, having the potential to become urban. The transformation had happened in Canterbury by the ninth century, at which point archaeological and documentary evidence reveal it to have been a densely-packed urban community. The mechanisms of this change are still open to debate.

In illuminating the transition to urban status, particular attention is currently being focused on the dynamic role of ecclesiastical institutions. The Church, with its extensive landed estates, acted as a landlord in the same way as any lay aristocrat. But there was an additional way in which the Church contributed very significantly to the commercialisation of the economy, and hence to the role of towns, and one to which a great deal more prominence should be given. For spiritual lordship entitled the Church to levy substantial sums from the laity. For Anglo-Saxon England, work is being done in particular on the role of minsters as pre-urban nuclei.[2]

Minsters were Anglo-Saxon churches which sustained a team of clergy serving very large parishes; the clergy were aristocratic and might be expected to draw on a wide area to satisfy both their intellectual and material demands. It is therefore significant that minsters were located on important routes, both by land and by water, as for example at

Oxford, which was one of a string of minsters along the Thames. For it was not just the demands of the elite but the way in which these demands were satisfied that contributed to the growth of towns. The conscious positioning of minsters on waterways implies that the minster clergy were alert to the possibilities of trade. The combination of position and personnel meant that minsters were able to generate growth around them, as they did from the ninth century onwards, with towns proper emerging by the tenth century. Debate now centres on whether the initiatives in making this change were taken by the aristocracy that occupied the pre-urban nuclei, or whether organic growth within the economy led to the creation of markets which the powerful then attempted to manipulate.

It is a debate that also relates to the function of the Anglo-Saxon burh. The creation of a network of burh fortifications by Alfred, King of Wessex and his successors in the late ninth and tenth centuries was made in response to first attacks by, and subsequently colonising invasions of, Vikings. The primary intention was to defend southern England. Hence not all places called burh were either suitable for, or intended as, trading centres. The burh also performed other functions, for example that of an administrative centre. But the intention with many of the foundations was also to channel and thus capitalise on trade, by directing it as far as possible to the burh. In pursuit of this, existing incipient urban settlements were brought into the network and mints were located within them to facilitate commerce. The coalescence of economic growth and its manipulation by those in power is evident also in the Danelaw, the area of North and East England under Viking control during the late ninth and tenth centuries. Vikings utilised what they found, orchestrating their colonisation from existing settlements, for example Thetford and Norwich. Excavations, particularly at York, have vividly demonstrated the expansion of trade and industry in what were systematically laid-out and densely occupied communities.[3]

In considering the foundation of the burh network by Alfred, Chris Dyer warns us against laying too much emphasis on the importance of deliberate foundations in quickening the pace of urban development, and against believing in a Wessex master plan for the foundation of towns.[4] As he points out, the correlation between Alfredian foundations and successful towns was not perfect. However, this does not diminish the significance of lordship in generating urban growth; rather that influence was exercised in a more oblique way. In tandem with the expanding economy of the ninth and tenth centuries, there were basic structural changes to the rural economy and rural society. This is an issue that will be returned to in more detail when discussing the foundation of twelfth-century towns, but basically it resulted from greater exploitation by landlords; the demands of lords fed the need for markets and towns where surplus products could be sold, so that peasants could raise money to pay taxes and other dues. More demands were being made by the Church as well as by secular powers. Between the tenth and the twelfth centuries there was a reorganisation of the Church at grass-roots level. The large parishes of the minsters were being subdivided, and a system of much smaller, local parishes developed. As with the minsters, the basic form of funding was through tithes, in theory a tenth of all produce (or for merchants and artisans, of profits). Tithes were to be paid by all laymen to the rector of their parish; a very substantial proportion of those paid in kind must have gone on to the market. In addition to this comprehensive system of taxation, the Church demanded payment for spiritual services, particularly those associated with rites of passage, from each parishioner. But as well as compulsory dues, there was a major element of voluntary giving. At a local level the commitment of powerful individuals and of groups of neighbours meant the mobilisation of yet more resources for the building and enhancement of parish churches.

Away from England, in other parts of the British Isles, there is minimal evidence of towns before the twelfth century. The only sure examples are the permanent Viking settlements made in Ireland from the tenth century onwards. How much of a novelty these Viking towns were is a matter of hot debate, turning largely on what is deemed to have constituted a town. Before the arrival of the Vikings, important Irish ecclesiastical centres, many of them monastic, acted as pre-urban nuclei, as for example at Kildare, Armagh or Glendalough. Dublin itself may possibly have incorporated the site of an existing monastery. Arguably ecclesiastical centres also had a political dimension, because of the close association of religious and secular power in Ireland, and this political dimension was likely to have been enhanced as Irish society moved towards more concentrated and centralised lordships in the eleventh and twelfth centuries.[5] Irish kings came to see the potential of Viking Dublin and Cork and had moved in to control the towns before the arrival of the Anglo-Normans in the late twelfth century. But a comparison of the subsequent history of Dublin with that of significant sacred pre-urban nuclei of Gaelic Ireland, such as Glendalough or Clonmacnoise, restates the point that sanctity and a powerful religious community on their own did not make a town; trade did.[6]

## Twelfth and Thirteenth Centuries

The factors encouraging the growth of towns in the ninth and tenth centuries were found in a far more potent combination throughout most of the British Isles from the late twelfth century, resulting in an explosion of town foundation and growth. Although much remains unclear it is possible to be a bit more positive about why a rapid expansion should have occurred at this juncture. The twelfth and thirteenth centuries were a time of rapid economic growth in Western Europe, take-off being particularly dramatic from the 1180s onwards. The population expanded, although within the British Isles it is only possible to give approximate figures for England to demonstrate this expansion: in 1180 there were perhaps 2–3 million people living in England; by 1330 there were perhaps 6 million.[7] The increase in population fed the growth of towns in a number of ways. More people meant the extension of cultivated land. Not only did agricultural output rise, but an increasing amount of produce was sold for cash. Specialisation in production encouraged this trend and fostered the proliferation of markets, both formal and informal. By the mid-fourteenth century there were three times as many formally constituted markets as there had been in 1200.[8] In addition there were numerous informal places of exchange which acted as unlicensed markets: the sale of goods in churchyards on Sundays, or at convenient crossroads.

By the early fourteenth century everyone in England was within daily reach of a market, indicative of a society which was rapidly becoming commercialised and where the sale of goods for cash and the purchase of essentials was the norm rather than the exception. It was a development driven not only by the increase in agricultural production but also by the pressure exerted by an expanding population. In the countryside there were a growing number of peasants who had no land, or only tiny holdings and who were dependent on wage labour. They, like the swelling population of the towns themselves, had to buy even basic foodstuffs in order to survive. It is the multitude of small-scale and local transactions that provided the essential framework for the growth of towns, and which formed the foundations on which a hierarchy of towns, offering increasingly specialised services, could be created.[9]

A further important factor in effecting these changes towards a more commercialised economy was the growth in the supply of money. Between 1186 and 1330 the amount of currency per head of population trebled in England. Particularly significant was the minting of smaller denominations; by the late thirteenth century the English were striking not only pennies, but halfpennies and farthings as well. It was predominantly English coinage that served the Scottish economy in the twelfth and thirteenth centuries, despite the introduction of mints to Scotland from the reign of David I (1124–53). The limited output of the Dublin mint was also supplemented by English coin. More currency smoothed the way to commercialisation, for if people have cash in hand they are not waiting for money to come in in order to spend it.[10] The importance of the money supply lay not only in the way it oiled small-scale transactions but also in the fact that the availability of credit was closely related to the amount of coin available; a fall in the amount of coin was accompanied by restrictions in credit. Hence monetarist historians place considerable emphasis on the increase in bullion supplies in explaining economic growth in the twelfth and thirteenth centuries.

But to describe an expanding economy does not give sufficient explanation for the extraordinarily rapid growth of towns in the late twelfth and thirteenth centuries. The point is made most strikingly by comparing England with Wales, Scotland and Ireland. There were no towns in Scotland and Wales before the twelfth century. In Ireland, as has been seen, almost the only settlements that everyone agrees to call towns were the Viking foundations along the coast. Nor indeed were there any towns in Northumberland before the arrival of the Normans. Towns in these places were quite plainly founded by lords. There is certainly evidence that sites were chosen in places ripe for economic exploitation. Perth, for example, developed so fast after its foundation as to suggest that it had already become a significant market place.[11] But the pre-urban nuclei of Scotland, Wales and Ireland, the defensive and monastic sites, did not on their own generate towns; these sites only developed under the influence of the Anglo-Normans.

As suggested earlier, the growth of towns was promoted by the social and economic relations inherent in feudal lordship. Seigneurial demand was first put forward as the key explanation for the take-off of French towns in the tenth and eleventh centuries by Duby.[12] This interpretation sees towns as agents of exploitation, vehicles through which the profits of the feudal economy could be translated into money that was needed to pay for the lavish lifestyle of consumption and warfare adopted by lords. Feudal lordship centred on the manor, which was not only or even primarily a territorial unit, but a package of territorial, fiscal and judicial rights, vested in the lord. For the lord of a manor (or a series of manors), a town not only provided profits from trade and rent, but also provided a place where peasant produce could be exchanged for the coin needed to pay the taxes and fines to which the lord considered himself entitled. Towns, then, far from being alien and subversive to the feudal society, were an integral part of it. In England, Anglo-Norman lords utilised the network of towns they already found in place. In Scotland, Wales and Ireland the Anglo-Normans introduced new forms of feudal lordship, based on the manor, and with it an appropriate restructuring of agriculture, so that the lord could realise his rights. Towns were planted at the same time to act both as market places, and as the administrative focus of the estate. Earl David of Huntingdon developed Dundee as the centre of his Tayside estates in Scotland. Further north, his foundation of Inverurie was planted in the Gairoch region, where rural production remained organised on traditional lines, a factor which contributed to the failure of Inverurie to develop beyond being a 'franchised hamlet'.[13] Towns epitomised the introduction of new economic and social relations and hence, as Davies has argued for Wales, could have an importance 'out of all proportion to their minuscule size'.[14]

The new dispensation extended to the spiritual sphere. The close association of the parochial system with other forms of feudal lordship is evident in Scotland, where David I introduced teinds (tithes) as part of the regularisation of Scottish parishes that went in parallel with the introduction of both feudal tenure and of burghs. Likewise in Ireland, the creation of a parochial system, which had begun in the early twelfth century, was vastly accelerated by the arrival of the Anglo-Normans, parishes being introduced with, and often made co-extensive with, manors. It is this common function that gives a unity to the foundation of towns throughout the British Isles: to take just one example, the Clare Earls of Hereford and Gloucester founded towns from Clare in Suffolk to Caerleon in Glamorgan, and from thence took off to Ireland, where they centred their lordship on towns such as Kilkenny.[15]

But although town foundation was intimately associated with Anglo-Norman influence, this is not to imply that the cultures of other groups within the British Isles were actively resistant to urban life. As we have seen, Irish kings had taken advantage of the potential of the Viking towns. A few of the Gaelic proto-towns, Armagh and Derry for example, were also developed by native Irish in imitation of Anglo-Norman towns, but they were a tiny minority among the overwhelming preponderance of Anglo-Norman foundations.[16] There were attempts by the Welsh princes, particularly those of Gwynedd, where a money economy was evolving in the thirteenth century, to copy the commercial success of

the Anglo-Normans. But no convincing network of towns was established and the vulnerability of native Welsh towns is evident in the fate of
Llanfaes, a settlement of perhaps 500, which was wiped out by Edward I
after the rebellion of 1284–85. In its place Edward built the castle of
Beaumaris, transferring the townspeople of Llanfaes, lock, stock and
barrel, to a new settlement, Newborough.[17]

Although towns have been discussed so far largely as expressions of
economic lordship, economic, social and political control were all intimately linked and reinforced one another. In the development of some
towns there was obviously an overtly political and military dimension,
which coloured their character. The invading Normans wasted parts of
key English towns so that they might build castles to pin down the native
population. In some instances, the overwhelming reason for the foundation of the town was as a statement of military power. This was true of
Carlisle, founded by Rufus in 1092 and sustained and shaped by English
royal policy on the borders far more than by its economic potential.[18] It
was particularly true of Wales, where towns were planted for strategic
reasons: most new towns were designed to serve the castles they clustered around as well as being intended to stimulate the local economy. A
massive castle could sustain a permanent urban community at its gates to
supply the needs of the garrison. Once the country was finally subjected
to English rule in the later middle ages, if the castle were rendered milit-
arily redundant, then the town might wither away, ultimately to become
a village, as happened at Trelech.[19]

The balance of priorities in the minds of lords who sought to exploit
the possibilities of the town determined the face that the town presented
to the world. The contrast between Welsh towns, built by conquerors,
and Scottish towns, the majority of which were first planted by a Scottish
king, makes the point. Scottish towns were not built with defences; they
seldom had walls and their gates were built to make a point about the
town's commercial significance. But too much should not be made of
the distinction between types of town on the strength of appearance:
walled or not walled, planted or organic; with planned gridiron streets
or with piecemeal growth, essentially all can be seen as manifestations
of lordship.

The years 1180–1250 saw the most rapid acceleration of urbanisation
under the active encouragement of lords. Not all of them flourished.
Foundations that overestimated or failed to consider the strength of the
local market never developed. Warrenmouth in Northumberland, with
its three miserable taxpayers in 1296, is one such foundation.[20] But

whereas most new foundations in England and Scotland did survive, the opposite was the case in Ireland, where most of the boroughs founded never made it to function as towns proper. This brings us to the question of how many towns there were in the British Isles. For most of the British Isles (excluding Scotland) the medieval urban network was at its fullest by c.1300. Counting towns is difficult, so only approximate numbers can be given. Failed boroughs, formal foundations that never got off the ground, have to be discounted, and equally the process of uncovering unofficial, unchartered towns is still going ahead. Estimates about the number of people who lived in these towns have to be tentative. There are only three points at which there is enough information to make even a hesitant calculation of the total urban population, and then only for England. These points are Domesday Book in 1086, the poll taxes of 1377, 1379 and 1381 and the subsidies of 1524/5. This makes particularly problematic the calculation of medieval urban populations at what was the time of their greatest extent, the beginning of the fourteenth century, for the poll taxes measure a population savagely reduced in the aftermath of the Black Death and subsequent plagues. Furthermore, comparison between these three attempts to exploit available resources is rendered more difficult because they were drawn up on a different basis to each other; each also manifests different forms of evasion and omission. Not only is it impossible to be certain of how many people lived in towns, but we have to be equally tentative about the proportion of the total population that towns included, given that every single variable involved in the calculation is open to dispute.

To take England first, in the late eleventh century there were c.110 towns, which, it has been estimated, accounted for about 10 per cent of the population. By 1300 the number of towns had grown to over 500. The vast majority of these had populations of under 2000; about 50 had populations of between 2000 and 5000 and possibly 20 of over 5000. Amongst these leading towns were regional centres already significant in Anglo-Saxon times, for example York, Winchester and Norwich, joined by some of the more spectacularly successful newcomers, in particular Newcastle upon Tyne and Boston. The difficulty of being certain as to just how crowded the largest towns were is evident from a recent recalculation of the evidence from Norwich, which has catapulted its population in the 1330s from 15 000 to 25 000.[21] London was considerably larger than all other towns, its population estimated as between 60 000 and 80 000 in the early fourteenth century.[22] The proportion of English people living in towns had also risen to perhaps 15–20 per cent of the total population by this date.

Whereas in England an urban hierarchy emerged over the twelfth and thirteenth centuries, in Wales and Scotland there was far less distinction between the smallest towns and those which seem to have acted as regional centres. In both countries the overwhelming majority of towns were very small. In Wales there were perhaps eighty towns by 1300, only three of which had a population of over 1000, Cardiff being the largest at c.2000.[23] In Scotland, 56 burghs had been created by 1306, again the majority very small; only Berwick (Scottish until its loss to the English in 1333), Edinburgh, Aberdeen, Dundee and Perth could number over 1000. It has been estimated that the urban population in the later middle ages was about 10 per cent of the total population of Scotland.[24] In Ireland, despite the fact that there had been over 250 foundations of towns, on the best estimate about 56 actually developed proper urban functions: the rest were no more than villages, boroughs only in name. Dublin was a very substantial town by the early fourteenth century, for which a population figure for upwards of 10 000 has been suggested. But a very incomplete hierarchy of towns developed in Ireland because effective colonisation was so patchy. In probably four-fifths of the country there was no ready access to a town, and in only two areas were genuine urban networks established, one around Dublin and the other around Waterford and New Ross. Even here the arrival of aggressive new players could undermine the fragile prosperity of an existing town, as New Ross undermined Wexford.[25]

## Fourteenth and Fifteenth Centuries

British towns underwent some fundamental changes in the fourteenth and fifteenth centuries for reasons that were both economic and political. In England the overall number of towns ceased to grow; the number of towns in Wales diminished. Scotland was different. There, in contrast to the rest of the British Isles, after the first flush of uban growth in the twelfth century, there had been very few towns founded in the thirteenth century, so that at a time when baronial boroughs were multiplying elsewhere, most Scottish burghs were under the direct control of the Crown: 38 of the 56 burghs in 1306 were royal. However, burghs of barony were founded in considerable numbers from the 1430s onwards and foundations continued unchecked throughout the sixteenth century.[26]

Given the generally depressing view presented until recently of the economy of late medieval Scotland, these foundations might seem rather surprising. They may suggest that the internal economy was not in such dismal shape as has hitherto been supposed. Certainly, the granting of the right to establish a burgh, given as a political favour, is unlikely to have persisted if these grants were completely useless. On the other hand, the creation of new burghs of barony may just have been the belated normalisation of marketing functions that had been in existence for some time. The apparently contradictory experience of Scotland is an indication of how murky some aspects of late medieval urbanisation remain. However, these reservations notwithstanding, there are good reasons for seeing the late thirteenth and first half of the fourteenth centuries as marking a significant turning point in the way that towns developed in the British Isles.

To take first changes in the economy, the growth which had characterised the thirteenth century over most of Europe ground to a halt by the 1290s, with stagnation sliding into what has been identified by some historians as a crisis by the early fourteenth century. How did this affect towns? To some extent large towns were sustained by their own momentum, the demand for goods and services made by their own inhabitants. But as already emphasised, essential to the urban network were the multitude of local transactions within the rural economy. Although the number of transactions had been growing during the period of expansion in the thirteenth century, the effect had been primarily to support a growing population. Whilst the richest peasants were able to profit from the more commercialised economy, the growth of the market had done next to nothing to increase the standard of living of the majority. They were dependent on ever-decreasing holdings and remained dangerously vulnerable. The commercial infrastructure was still immature and 'uneven in quality', meaning that markets were very volatile.[27] As a result crises in the rural economy, for example those brought about by harvest failure, could have a devastating effect locally, pushing a greater proportion of people to the margins of subsistence, curtailing the demand for urban products and ultimately bringing starvation to the landless, dependent as they were on the market for food.

The swollen towns of the early fourteenth century probably also included a mass of underemployed marginals on the precarious edge of existence, many of them desperate migrants from an overpopulated countryside. The position was altered dramatically and hideously in 1348–49 by the mortality of the Black Death; nor were population levels able to recover for over 150 years owing to repeated visitations of plague. English towns lost approximately a third of their populations, and the impact of plague seems to have been as great in Wales, though possibly rather less in Scotland. But smaller towns were not necessarily weaker towns. Nor was the urban network dismantled. Britnell emphasises that despite the huge fall in population in England, the overall distribution of towns did not change fundamentally. While village markets, and villages themselves, went to the wall in great numbers, towns did not disappear; they had become a permanent feature.[28]

The same generalisation seems to hold for Scotland and to a lesser extent for Wales, where, as will be seen, towns do seem to have been rather more vulnerable. What did change were patterns of supply and demand. The reduction of population brought a redistribution of incomes. A smaller number of tenants meant that not only did some peasant holdings become larger, but the tenants could also bargain for lower rents. Equally, a shortage of labour brought about rising wage rates for both agricultural and industrial workers. What has to be balanced is whether this increase in the spending power of individuals was adequate to compensate for other powerful factors which depressed the economy: the overall fall in output, exacerbated periodically by severe problems with the money supply. In drawing up a hypothetical balance sheet it is a mistake to treat the 150 years following the Black Death as a unity. Initially, greater per capita income and changing patterns of demand brought prosperity to towns in the later fourteenth century, but circumstances seem to have become much more difficult in the fifteenth century, particularly in the mid-fifteenth century, with recovery flickering into life by the late fifteenth or early sixteenth centuries. But examination of urban fortunes in the fifteenth century makes another point abundantly clear: there were huge variations in local experience. The debate which is currently being pursued as to whether towns declined in the later middle ages needs therefore to take account of both time and place.[29]

Most of the pessimism about the health of the urban sector attaches to the fifteenth century. Evidence has been amassed from diminished corporate income, falling rent rolls, vacant holdings and contracting trade to show that both major centres such as York and middle-rank towns such as Grimsby ran into deep crisis. Hatcher takes a particularly gloomy view of urban prospects in the mid-fifteenth century as the economy sank into the depths of the mid-century recession. Although admitting to signs of urban recovery from the 1470s onwards, he remains suspicious of the appearance of prosperity in all major provincial towns in the late fifteenth and early sixteenth centuries. He cites as one particularly dramatic example Coventry's strong showing in sixteenth-century urban league tables, with the reality of 'desolation' found in Phythian-Adams's detailed account of the crisis that overtook the city in the early sixteenth century.[30] Bailey is equally pessimistic about the outlook for small towns in the later middle ages, as competition between them grew for a share in a shrinking market. His comparison of the fortunes of Buntingford and Standon in Hertfordshire shows the former prospering at the latter's expense from the later fourteenth century onwards. Buntingford was a newer settlement and part of its appeal probably lay in the fact that it was a 'peasant-led initiative' lacking the expensive oversight of a lord.[31] For Bailey, seigneurial jurisdiction and the privileges of urban status had become a liability.

Chris Dyer is far more upbeat about the success of small towns in the later middle ages. He argues that, with some regional exceptions, the majority of small towns in England either managed to sustain their populations between the late fourteenth century and the early sixteenth century, or in some instances actually show an increase.[32] Equally, the proportion of people living in English towns was as great or greater in 1500 than it had been in the early fourteenth century. The optimists also argue that in England, in terms of taxable wealth, towns were accounting for a greater share of the national total by the early sixteenth century than they had been in the early fourteenth. The figures on which this assessment is based, derived from a comparison between the tax returns of 1334 and those of 1524/5, have been subject to fierce critical scrutiny. The 1334 returns are deemed to be particularly unreliable because of underassessment and evasion. But however extreme this underassessment, it is still impossible to juggle the figures to make towns out as having declined in wealth in comparison to rural areas between the early fourteenth and early sixteenth centuries.

However, and again this can only be demonstrated for England, the distribution of this wealth between towns and between regions was radically different by 1500. When changes in taxable wealth are mapped county by county, it becomes evident that southern English counties were markedly increasing in prosperity, to the detriment of those in the Midlands and the North. In general terms Alan Dyer concludes that 'towns with problems lie in agricultural regions suffering parallel losses of people and wealth'.[33] The intimate connection between the prosperity of the town and the prosperity of the urban hinterland is a point that will be picked up again in the next chapter, as will consideration of one of the major contributory factors to the prosperity of the most flourishing areas, the growth of the cloth industry. It is the small cloth-making towns which come from nowhere to figure so significantly in Alan Dyer's league tables of urban population and prosperity by the early sixteenth century. Given the complexity of all these changes, and the conflicting evidence, it seems at this stage more judicious to talk of urban realignment in late medieval England than urban decline.

But the question of the relative decline or growth of towns in the later middle ages was not just a matter of economics, and this is particularly the case for Wales and Ireland. As we have seen, economic growth had been linked with the exercise of power from the point at which towns begin to emerge. In Wales, Ireland and Scotland, the late thirteenth and early fourteenth centuries were marked by political events which changed significantly the relationship of these countries to the English Crown, and this in turn had an impact on the place of towns both in their own localities and in terms of their role within their respective kingdoms and principalities.

In Wales the late thirteenth century saw the definitive conquest of the country, with Edward I's onslaught in response to the claims of Llewelyn ap Gruffudd. In the colonisation that followed the conquest of 1282–83, the privileges of existing towns were reinforced and Welsh settlements such as Criccieth were absorbed into the system of English boroughs.[34] Inevitably the extensive settlement had an impact on the function of towns. As we have seen, the different political objectives, control of a colonised territory, meant that during the fourteenth century some castles whose function had been purely strategic became redundant, and their boroughs withered. For other towns the more stable conditions brought prosperity: the economic base of Brecon and Ruthin, and in the case of Carmarthen the administrative significance of the town, made it possible for these places to grow in the later middle ages.

But the single most important change in Welsh towns concerned ethnic identity. It was only following the revolt of 1295 that boroughs became explicitly the preserve of the English colonists, and that for the first time there was overt legalised discrimination against the Welsh.[35] The Welsh were forbidden to live in the English boroughs, to trade outside them or to carry arms when within them. It was during the course of the fourteenth century that boroughs took steps to enforce this discrimination, making themselves centres of Englishness, and by doing so also making themselves the targets of Welsh resentment. Because it was largely the English who had benefited from the boroughs, it was specifically the boroughs that were attacked in the last major Welsh revolt, that of Owain Glyn Dŵr, in 1400. The resulting vindictive legislation was to reinforce ethnic divisions for generations.

The attacks by Glyn Dŵr proved materially devastating for some urban communities, with some small towns disappearing altogether. Soulsby argues that flourishing towns were the exception rather than the rule by the fifteenth century.[36] All Welsh towns remained small; no proper hierarchy developed. Hence the picture of a depressed urban sector which is so contentious for English towns seems to attach itself more readily to the late medieval Welsh landscape.

Whereas in Wales the late fourteenth century saw the extension of colonisation, in Ireland the reverse was the case. Colonisation had always been patchy in Ireland, and with pressure from the native Irish growing from the 1270s onwards, towns in west and even central Ireland found themselves isolated. This isolation did not constitute a threat to urban existence, but it did mean that the function of the town and its economic rationale changed. Gaelicised Anglo-Norman lords adopted the social and economic organisation of the Irish, with wealth derived from cattle and with rural power bases, dispensing with the need for a network of small local markets. Hence though Anglo-Irish and Gaelic lords utilised established towns, the emphasis shifted even more significantly to the ports, through which those in power could export livestock and fish and import luxuries. Further than this, towns became Irish-speaking, and as Irish law and custom were adopted, the physical face of the town changed also. Tower houses were built to accommodate merchants who had adopted the style of the rural Irish, and who used the basements of these secure dwellings as warehouses. The changes were profound, but Clarke questions whether it is accurate to call this adaptation of Irish towns decline, preferring to see it as a manifestation of a new and possibly more dynamic form of economic organisation.[37]

Finally, in Scotland, Edward I's invasion and virtual conquest of the country between 1296 and 1305 inspired the Wars of Independence. By 1328 in the Treaty of Edinburgh, England was forced to recognise the separate existence of the kingdom of Scotland, though war continued until the 1330s, when the outbreak of the Hundred Years War with France put paid to English attempts to reconquer Scotland. Scottish independence ensured that the two monarchies continued to develop in different ways in the later middle ages. The centralisation of the English state, and of the English legal system, which had been undertaken in the thirteenth century, was consolidated in the later middle ages. In comparison Scotland remained far less centralised and this placed Scottish towns in a different relationship to the Crown. Amongst the towns themselves the most significant reorientation of rank came with the loss of Berwick to the English in 1333 (save for a brief period when it was recaptured at the end of the fifteenth century). Berwick had been Scotland's chief exporting town: its trade now moved to Edinburgh and resulted in the rapid growth of that city to a position of complete economic as well as political dominance among Scottish towns.

Towns were an integral part of the economy and society in England at the end of the twelfth century, and were becoming established in a somewhat more piecemeal fashion in other parts of the British Isles. Although the common motivation behind town foundation and the fostering of urban growth in the twelfth and thirteenth centuries gives a point of comparison from which to start, the divergent experience of towns over the twelfth to early sixteenth centuries draws attention to the very considerable changes in function in individual towns. It is these functions, economic, political and social, that the succeeding chapters go on to examine.

# 2

# THE URBAN ECONOMY

It is as well to begin a chapter on the urban economy with a reminder that the activities we associate with towns, marketing and manufacture went on in rural locations and continued to do so to a very considerable extent throughout the middle ages. There was of course a great deal of rural industry: quarrying, mining, smelting of iron and tin, charcoal burning, village-based smiths and carpenters, part-time weaving and spinning in rural households. The scale of extra-urban manufacture varied with place and time, but there is no indication of it diminishing in quantity by the fifteenth century. On the contrary, as will be seen, one of the difficulties faced by some towns in the fifteenth century was the extent to which they were facing a new set of challenges from rural manufacturing. In tandem with all this industry, there was an active marketing network in the countryside. Goods were regularly bought from rural producers at source or in unlicensed trading places as well as at recognised village markets. Most of the informal exchange among peasants has inevitably gone unrecorded, but larger transactions can be traced more readily. Sizeable households made direct bulk purchases of food and other basic essentials from rural suppliers, as did merchants engaged in long-distance trade. Artisans and small-scale dealers made sorties out of town to sell at unlicensed venues likely to catch the rural poor: the practice of selling 'at doors of church' on Sunday, though theoretically banned from the thirteenth century onwards, was still prevalent in the fifteenth.

Goods were exchanged at annual fairs as well as through the network of weekly markets. Most towns, well aware of the commercial potential of fairs, acquired the right to hold one; the Scottish kings endeavored to restrict fairs to towns altogether, in order to foster the growth of newly founded boroughs. So, for example, the horse and oxen fairs were central to the prosperity of Dunblane.[1] But important regional fairs did not have to be located in towns; they might be held in villages that made convenient venues, particularly for the gathering of livestock, and like Corbridge fair in the north of England, they might survive well past the middle ages because of their manifest usefulness.[2] Fairs ranged in scale and attraction from the very local, through regional fairs such as Corbridge and Dunblane, to the great fairs which were until the fourteenth century the key venues for international trade: Winchester, Boston, Stamford, St Ives (Cambridgeshire), King's Lynn. A large centre was not a requirement for a successful international fair, and the St Ives fair was hosted by a very modest town. What the fairs provided were concentrated facilities, unfettered by normal trading restrictions; in their heyday they were particularly valuable for alien merchants coming to England to buy wool, gathered at the fairs from all parts of the British Isles.

The great fairs were only likely to lose their position at the top of the market when denizen merchants could offer a year-round availability of the kinds of goods that had been offered for sale at fairs. This depended in turn both on the scale and regularity of their business warranting the holding of large stocks, and on the development of sufficiently sophisticated credit arrangements to allow for a sedentary merchant class to emerge. By the early fourteenth century these changes had taken place and the great fairs dwindled in significance. However they were not yet wholly done for; the changing trading patterns of the fifteenth century saw something of a revival, particularly in the flourishing fair at Stourbridge in Cambridgeshire. So the urban market has to be seen in the context of all these other outlets, and historians no longer consider the trade of towns in isolation from that of their rural hinterlands; rather, urban growth is seen as an aspect of the commercialisation of society as a whole.

The town slotted into the network of village markets, and itself offered an outlet for local produce on a fixed day or days during the week. But a town also provided year-round facilities for wholesaling and retailing, six days a week, and in an emergency, on Sundays. The more substantial the town, the wider the variety of goods and services permanently on offer. The smallest towns, those struggling to maintain their position as towns at all, might only be blessed with part-time artisans and traders who had not the resources to stockpile raw materials. This was probably the case with some of the smaller Scottish towns founded in the twelfth century, and undoubtedly was the case with the vast majority of Irish towns, which were, in fact, no more than chartered villages.

A small town proper needed to be able to support the majority of inhabitants in non-agrarian pursuits. Typical of such a town was Halesowen, where in the late thirteenth century there were about thirty-five separate non-agrarian occupations; about half of these involved food processing or dealing in food, and half manufacture. Some particular specialisms did develop even at a very local level. Stratford-upon-Avon was on the border of two very different rural landscapes, respectively woodland and arable, and the townspeople seem to have capitalised on this by specialising in the sale of timber and of agricultural implements.[3] A larger town offered a more exciting array of products, with provincial capitals such as Norwich already having nearly seventy different occupations by 1300. As well as the massed ranks of shoemakers and tanners, butchers, fishmongers and innkeepers, weavers and smiths that were needed to service basic needs, Norwich offered specialists: goldsmiths, lorimers (who cast the metal parts of harness), needlers, apothecaries, surgeons, a perfumer and a growing number of professionals, ecclesiastical and lay.[4]

Most of the evidence we have about occupational diversity comes from English towns. There is not the documentary evidence for Scottish towns before the fifteenth century to give an impression of the range of occupations practised there, but even by the early sixteenth century, Edinburgh, with 20 separately identified crafts, does not appear to have been able to support a very diverse economy. Even if the individual rich were able to get most of what they wanted through Edinburgh, the demand from the mass market was not able to sustain the sort of specialists available in Norwich or, even more dramatically different, London. The list of nearly 200 crafts practising in late medieval London includes the entrancingly minute: the agletmaker producing tags for shoelaces, the kerchief lavanders offering specialist washing services, the seal engravers.[5]

What has been described is the emergence of a hierarchy of towns, though a hierarchy that was more clearly defined in England than it was in Scotland, Ireland or Wales. Currently some medieval historians are showing interest in applying the central place theory of urban geographers in explaining how this hierarchy worked. Central place theory proposes an ordered relationship between towns, with a hierarchy based on function rather than population. Regional centres will have the biggest sphere of influence; they provide the widest variety of specialised goods and services and they can attract business from a very wide area because of the value of the commodities available, hence they are the centres of long-distance trade. They act as distribution centres, serving as collection points for goods from towns at the next stage down in the urban hierarchy, and in return sending out to those towns goods imported in long-distance trade. Intermediate towns are themselves 'lower-order' distribution centres, acting as a link between the regional centres and the local market. The entire marketing structure is, in this model, integrated into a series of interlocking networks.

This theoretical framework cannot be made to apply with too great an exactness; each hierarchy will have its own unique quality, a uniqueness that has led to the theory having an 'ambivalent reception' among medievalists.[6] But for Chris Dyer central place theory does provide an 'appropriate framework' for understanding the role of the mature network of market towns that was established in England by 1300, as long as local variations as to how this hierarchy operated are given proper recognition.[7] The more detailed consideration of different sectors of the economy later in this chapter will highlight some of the factors that contributed to shifts and realignments in the urban hierarchy during the course of the middle ages.

One difficulty with a model which geographers have constructed on the basis of the ideal modern state with clear national frontiers, is that it needs to take into account the far less well defined political boundaries of the middle ages. Within Ireland there was no clear-cut boundary between the Gaelic and Anglo-Norman or English settlements; this patchy colonisation meant that only two rather fragile urban networks emerged, and it is doubtful whether either of these can be regarded as a hierarchy. Almost all of Ireland's external trade until the late fifteenth century went through England (although trade with Ireland was in fact taxed as foreign trade, the only concession being that English subjects could pay lower levels of customs). There was a little traffic from Ireland to Welsh ports; most shipping from Wexford, Waterford and Cork went to Bristol. Bristol took a controlling interest in Welsh as well as Irish trade and hence the Severn estuary formed tightly knit trading area. This was one of the reasons that no genuine urban hierarchy emerged in Wales either; the regional centres that exerted most influence over Welsh towns lay over the border in England: Bristol in the south, Shrewsbury and Chester in central and north Wales respectively.

Between England and Scotland, in the west Carlisle had a natural hinterland north of what became fixed as the border, whilst on the east coast Berwick was the chief outlet for border wool and Scotland's main port until its loss to the English in 1333. Even after this date, owing to its anomalous customs arrangements, it continued to attract wool exports from both sides of the border until the general slump in the wool market in the late fourteenth century.[8] But the example of Berwick does serve as a reminder that the creation of regional hierarchies was not only a matter of economics. It was politics which meant that Edinburgh and not Berwick became the chief centre of long-distance trade in Scotland in the later middle ages.

## The Regulation of Trade

The specialised goods and services offered by towns came at a price. By concentrating trade as far as possible in towns, it also made it very much easier to tax. So for the lord to reap the financial benefits of a town it was necessary to enlist the support of the townspeople by offering them a package of privileges that gave them a vested interest in channelling trade through the urban market. Burgesses were to be attracted to the town by a number of devices that gave them the commercial edge on foreigns, the term that applied to anyone from outside the town. Burgesses were allowed to retail freely anywhere in the town, whereas non-burgesses were restricted to selling retail in the market. Burgesses could trade free of toll, whereas non-burgesses would have to pay on commodities brought in for sale. Levies were made sometimes on the seller, sometimes on the buyer, sometimes on both. The list of goods on which toll could be charged was extensive, but was meant to exclude goods bought for ordinary domestic consumption – though creative use could be made of this latter category. In the mid-thirteenth century the bailiff of Stamford was suspicious of the destination of large quantities of bread taken out of the town ostensibly 'in alms for the souls of the dead around Stamford' and charged toll on it; however, this bailiff was altogether a vindictive man and had shown himself on other occasions ready to toll anything at all that came through the gate.[9]

Dealings in certain commodities were sometimes entirely restricted to burgesses; most often this applied to wool, woolfells and cloth, though in thirteenth-century Exeter the list ran to wine, spices, salt and dyes as well.[10] The monopolies of the urban burgesses could be extended into the countryside, as was usually the case in Wales; the burgesses of Caernarfon, for example, had exclusive rights to trade in an area extending for an eight-mile radius round the town.[11] Royal burghs in Scotland were given even more extensive privileges, being allocated a broad trading zone throughout which the burgesses had a monopoly of trade in wool, fells and hides. Whether the most sweeping privileges could be sustained has to be doubted. Dundee, for example, claimed all trade in wool, fells and hides throughout the Sheriffdom of Forfar; but the success of the small town of Coupar Angus, though specifically banned from trespassing on Dundee's monopoly, serves as a reminder of the amount of unlicensed trade that was carried on.[12]

The burgesses of certain privileged towns also obtained the right to trade free of toll either in other named towns or in towns throughout the kingdom, though some of these grants must have been difficult to effect in practice. The twelfth-century burgesses of Devizes were given sweeping rights to freedom from toll by Matilda, grateful for the town's consistent loyalty to her in the war against Stephen in the mid-twelfth century. One cannot help feeling that there would have been a fair degree of scepticism in places where traders turned up claiming that they were from Devizes and were not going to pay anything.

The more frequent use of written records from the thirteenth century onwards enabled merchants to carry validations of the privileges they claimed and meant also that towns could keep regularly updated records of just who was allowed what. This also enabled adjudication to be made where exemptions conflicted, for example where one town claimed a royal grant to exact toll from everyone and another a royal grant to its burgesses to trade free of toll anywhere; in all instances the older of the two grants was given priority. Inevitably the kaleidoscope of different exemptions and monopolies led to hundreds of disputes and meant that towns had to work hard to defend themselves against dominant neighbours. The men of Wells were not exceptional in taking their charter of liberties on tour to maintain their rights against their overdominant neighbour Bristol.[13] All in all, the effect of granting of exemptions to burgesses does seem to have meant that it was those at the bottom of the pile that tended to pay tolls: peasants and dealers from other small towns, those characterised as 'miserable creatures' by the Edinburgh burgesses.[14]

Even though the primary intention of these privileges was to disadvantage outsiders, access to them was not open to all who lived within the town. Although initially the status of burgess and the freedoms that that entailed was a general grant to all those who held property in the town, it usually came to be a restricted category in the gift of those who controlled the town, and acquired at a cost. The process by which this happened is obscure, and is discussed in more detail in Chapter 3. The

effect was that the freemen of the town, those who enjoyed the full benefits of the trading privileges, were usually a minority. Other town dwellers
might buy the right to some of these privileges on a temporary basis,
for example, the right to sell retail through the purchase of an annual
licence. The advantages of burgessship could be strictly tied to residence, as in Berwick after its return to the English in 1333, in order to
ensure a stable and loyal population.[15] But residence in the town was not
always compulsory for the privileged; there was a class of burgesses 'de
vento' in Wales, those traders who moved around a great deal and who
needed a number of bases. Elsewhere access to privileged trading could
be obtained, at a cost, by joining the town's guild merchant, if it had one.
It was an option taken up by a broad swathe of aspiring rural entrepreneurs, both gentry and peasants, as well as dealers from other towns. The
majority of those in the foreigns guild at Shrewsbury were in fact villagers
from places within a 20-mile radius of the town.[16]

Urban dealers capitalised further on their existing advantages by
going out into the countryside to earmark supplies at source. This was a
necessary part of a successful enterprise and, indeed, was the basis for
the blanket monopolies imposed around Scottish and some Welsh
towns. What was not acceptable was to use local knowledge to the disadvantage of fellow burgesses and to the advantage of foreigns. It was
regarded as particularly scandalous if an attempt was made to corner the
market in a specific commodity and thus force up prices in times of scar-
city. Hence the constant attempts to foil forestalling, that is, the purchase
of goods outside the limits of the town specifically to avoid urban regulations controlling supply. One Wylkyson 'maximus foristallator' operating in the vicinity of Aberdeen in the early fifteenth century seems to
have been guilty of outflanking his fellow merchants; he was accused of
selling cattle and hides directly southwards, avoiding the inconvenience
and cost of taking them first to Aberdeen.[17] More sinister was the con-
federacy of the shameless Simon Broke, sometime bailiff and MP for
Gloucester, formed in 1386 specifically to monopolise the purchase of
grain coming into Tewkesbury market by road or by river.[18]

Although the privileged leaders of the urban community, like Simon
Broke, did exploit the market to the limit, their behaviour was condemned by public opinion. For although the townspeople protected
their privileges fiercely against outsiders, there was a strong sense of the
necessity of ensuring a semblance of equal access to commodities arriving in the town. In Aberdeen corporate purchases were made of shiploads of basic produce such as grain and salt, which were then sold on a

non-profit-making basis to the townspeople. Provision was made for ordinary householders to have access to food at fair prices before the bulk buyers swung into action, so that, again in Aberdeen, the sale of oat-cakes was banned altogether, and merchants were forbidden to buy oat-meal in bulk, in order that there should be enough of this basic foodstuff for the poor.[19]

Another way in which the urban authorities feared that prices might be hiked was through the actions of regrators and hucksters. Here the people being targeted were at the bottom end of the social scale; very often they were women. Regrators and hucksters were integral to the urban economy for they acted as redistributors within the town, hawk-ing goods outside the market, often from inns and taverns. Hilton has drawn the proper attention of historians to the scale of the trade con-ducted in this way, both in large towns and in small – and also to the fact that it was very easy for the civic authorities to exploit the existence of hucksters and regrators on the margins of legality by regularly present-ing them for contravention of the growing number of urban by-laws.[20]

In all this legislation a suspicion of the profit-making middleman comes across, but given that those who prospered most out of urban society were making money out of being middlemen, there was a built-in potential for tension in interpreting the rules. Equally, the standard of living that the rule-setters regarded as the basic minimum to which they were entitled was almost inevitably rather higher than that considered adequate for the majority. The unfair way in which access to commodities was in practice restricted, or the market manipulated, comes out regular-ly in complaints made against urban elites who forestalled or engrossed trade, or those sectional interests which, by the fifteenth century, mono-polised common land for the pasturing of cattle on a commercial basis.

One of the things that has to be constantly borne in mind when consid-ering the relationship between town and country is the potential for all this regulation to drive away trade. Whereas the advantages for the priv-ileged burgesses are clear, the small dealer who bore the brunt of the tolls and scrutiny of the urban officials was likely to feel that the urban market place had its limitations. On the other hand the plus side of urban regulation was the battery of legislation in place to try and pre-vent underhand practices. Regulations relating to weights and measures went back to the tenth century in England. They were elaborated on at both a national and local level during the course of the middle ages, introduced into all other parts of the British Isles and supplemented by a broad spectrum of other rules controlling the standard and quality of goods for sale. On balance the convenience in access to customers and the relative security offered by a well-policed urban market probably sufficiently compensated for the costs involved.

## Urban Occupations

Towns acted as a draw not only for goods but also for people. It would seem to be the case that towns were unable to reproduce themselves, death rates outstripping birth rates, so that in order to stay the same size, let alone grow, they were dependent on migration. Some of this migration was a move of desperation; movement into the swollen towns of the early fourteenth century by landless peasants exchanged one form of poverty for another. But apart from the fact that the town was probably a great deal more interesting to live in than the country, it did offer greater potential employment and at times certainly offered better wage rates than the country. This applies particularly to the late fourteenth century, when shortage of labour after the Black Death, coupled with rising living standards, meant that the openings for skilled employment within towns multiplied, enticing people away from the countryside.

The rest of this chapter considers the three areas in which livings could be made within towns: marketing, manufacture and service industry. However, some preliminary cautionary remarks are called for in order to avoid categorising townspeople too rigidly into one or other of these sectors. Medieval administrators showed a growing predilection for pigeonholing people by their primary occupation. Whereas in the twelfth century only a minority of people were so identified, by the fifteenth century in England the majority had a specific occupational title, as indeed was required by statute.[21] However, this precision is in fact rather misleading. People came to towns because of the variety of opportunities that the town offered for making money and it would be unreal not to expect them to maximise these opportunities; a versatile individual could readily slip from one skill to another. Thomas Littleton of Westminster was variously a doctor, parchmentmaker, scrivener and sergeant at law; the Welsh cloth worker Simon ap Madog was moonlighting as a harpist in 1416; John Edwyn, a York chaplain, eked out what was presumably a thin income by making bowstrings.[22]

More significant than the versatility of the individual, however, was the fact that the main industrial unit was the household, and the overall income of the household was unlikely to come from a single source, though one particular skill very often predominated. Households diversified into as many money-making schemes as presented themselves, licit and illicit. One of the best ways of illustrating this point is to look at the victualling industry, which encompassed all three facets of urban enterprise, marketing, manufacture and service industry, and which was often carried on as a secondary enterprise within the household economy. There were full-time victuallers, but the bulk of urban drink and a fair proportion of eatables were prepared and traded by small-scale and part-time operators. In a town such as Westminster, admittedly a place particularly geared to consumption because of the amount of official business there, it is plausibly claimed that in the later middle ages the 'greater part of the inhabitants were involved in victualling'.[23]

The brewing of ale is the part-time activity that can most easily be pinned down, because its sheer ubiquity made it a useful source of revenue; lists of brewers fined for breaking regulations are so commonly found as to suggest they were an unofficial form of tax, a licensing system. Such lists reveal the very high proportion of women brewers: a 1509 census of Aberdeen brewers lists 80 per cent of them as wives of burgesses.[24] Given official preference for fixing responsibility on the male head of the household, where we find, as in Nottingham, that the brewers included a cordwainer (shoemaker), a clerk, a cook and a cooper among others, it seems likely that the female members of the household were doing the brewing. This was certainly the case with Emma Stayngate, the widow of a prosperous York saddler. She left her brewing equipment and the use of her brewery to Agnes Paponham, presumably a servant or a friend, on condition that Agnes gave four gallons of best ale from each brewing to the poor, from the door from which she customarily sold. It was the wives of the more prosperous, merchants, rich artisans and professionals, who featured most strongly as brewers, having the time and resources to invest. But the trade had its raffish, even criminal, end: Lucy, a London tailor's servant who worked as a brewer and aleseller, was accused in 1276 of beating to death a female rival.[25] Poorer alewives did not brew for themselves, but bought in ale to sell; their retail outlets might offer in addition those useful service industries, prostitution and fencing of stolen goods.

Less easy to track down than brewing, but probably equally useful as a commercial sideline, was the provision of accommodation. Though by the fifteenth century in London wealthy visitors were expecting a private room, elsewhere, and lower on the social scale, they could be stacked into the spare rooms of any reasonably sized building: John

Stubbs, a York barber, could sleep 36 in his six-bedroomed house. Inevitably inns became centres of trading; so, for example, the bridge-wardens of Rochester Bridge were allowed their expenses for several visits to taverns 'for buying timber'. Hostellers used their connections to diversify in many directions, like the Exeter hosteller who at various times was also a cordwainer, a dealer, a brewer and, at least by repute, a brothel keeper; John Stubbs of York, as well as housing and shaving his customers, brewed ale and dealt in malt and barley.[26] The appearance of growing numbers of innkeepers in urban records in the later middle ages is therefore probably due as much to a change in the way people described themselves than to an actual growth in innkeeping. The same cautious approach to job ascription has to be observed when putting together the overall occupational profile of any medieval town. Having made this proviso, the twentieth-century historian, like the medieval administrator, feels compelled to impose some sense of order on the evidence – hence the arrangement of the rest of the chapter. But it should always be borne in mind that the same people could be involved in each category.

## Marketing and Trade: Local and Long-distance

*Local trade*

Local markets served small-scale operators, those with relatively small amounts of produce to sell and who were not lavish and extravagant in their purchases. Stress is now being laid by historians on just how significant these small-scale transactions were in the commercialisation of the economy. Within the countryside production for the market was not only characteristic of landlords; equally, if not more significant, was peasant commodity production. And it was that portion of peasant output destined for sale and not personal consumption that gave rise to the multiplicity of local markets. The expansion of the number of transactions at this level in turn fuelled the growth of towns, though we should be careful to remember that there was no smooth and seamless progression towards a commercialised economy, and that the effective working of the market developed unevenly.

Records of debt registered in English borough or manorial courts have been used to map how far people travelled to their local market; what is emerging is that a normal journey was some 6–7 miles (or about

10 km) – 'uncannily close' to the figure of 6.6 miles used by thirteenth-century lawyers as a basis for calculating a reasonable distance between rival markets.[27] Loughborough can be taken as typical of one such local market. It was a small town of under 1000 in population, not formally consitituted as a borough but sufficiently well established to have four distinct market precincts, for mercery, butchery, drapery and ironmongery, serving a hinterland of a radius of about seven miles.[28] The zone of influence would be more extensive for a small town which could offer a particular specialism, as Stratford did with its implements and building materials. Stratford's area of influence was nevertheless moulded by competition from other nearby market centres; hence it served an oval-shaped hinterland, extending for 15 miles at its furthest point, and aligned along the main roads out of the town to the north-west and south-east.[29]

The overwhelming preponderance of small-scale dealings in the local market is underlined by the relative indifference of large institutions or very wealthy individuals to the market on their doorstep. King's College Cambridge in the fifteenth century bought from venues as distant as Salisbury and Winchester; it obtained fish from Stourbridge fair and from London. London also supplied them with consumer durables such as bells and pewter. What they did not do was to use Cambridge as their main source of supply.[30] The servants of religious or wealthy lay households were more regular and useful local customers than their masters. But whilst local trade was the lifeblood of small towns, it also made up the majority of transactions in larger regional centres. In Exeter, which by the late fourteenth century had a population of c.3000, the majority of those who appeared in debt cases before the borough courts lived within six miles of the city. It was also the case that these people registered the smallest debts, often representing petty loans or small-scale purchases made on credit.

With all these generalisations it should of course be remembered that the evidence largely comes from the more densely populated southern half of England and can not necessarily be readily translated to the more sparsely populated areas of the British Isles, where small towns perforce had a larger hinterland; the thickening Scottish urban network of the later middle ages may be marking out the informal points of exchange that had operated within these wider hinterlands up to the latter part of the fifteenth century.

Local trade was not just a matter of rural producers coming to sell their goods in an urban market. For townspeople, the incentive to become wholesalers, even on a very small scale, was a powerful one, because money was to be made far more readily in distribution than in manufacture. Thus we find, involved in the marketing of produce, men and women with all sorts of craft and occupational ascriptions, including members of the clergy who can be found acting on their own initiative and for their own profit. It was only in the largest towns that a distinctive merchant class emerged. In small towns there may have been the occasional merchant, but a great deal of trade was carried on by people who were artisans as well as dealers.

Attention has already been drawn to the innkeepers who dealt in grain; bakers and brewers also, naturally enough, moved in as middlemen in the local grain trade. Even in a larger town, such as Colchester, one that handled a fair amount of long-distance trade and acted as a regional distributive centre, the local grain market seems to have been handled by small-scale dealers and artisans. An alleged conspiracy to avoid toll on grain in 1334 implicated three women and four husband-and-wife partnerships, none of whom were among Colchester's leading merchants.[31] This last example is a necessary reminder of the importance of women as small-scale dealers, but it is not always possible to have access to the extent of their activities. In Loughborough Postles found that women appeared less in records of debt litigation than men, though their dealings may have been masked behind those of a named, male partner. The Loughborough women debtors also accounted for smaller sums, and the impression given is that even at the level of the local market they were operating at something of a disadvantage.

One potentially very lucrative way into the wholesale market, and one that needs more attention, was by negotiating the sale of tithes. Urban clergy might act as entrepreneurs in this respect: one of the canons of York Minster, John de Warenne, paid £30 a year in the early 1330s for the right to sell the tithes of a fellow clergyman, the rector of Dewsbury. But it was also a way into the market for enterprising laymen and women. This was the tactic of Robert le Walker of Ruthin, who leased the tithes of the local rectory, paying the rector £24 for them and presumably making rather more for himself when the produce was sold. A syndicate of York artisans, including a smith, a dyer, a baker and a butcher, used the same route into the market, paying one of the Minster prebendaries £8 in exchange for collecting a portion of his tithes.[32] Butchers were in fact particularly well placed, if they could extend their activities into cattle dealing, because of the demand for animal by-products from so many different crafts. Their position was strengthened in the later middle ages as standards of living rose for the majority in the aftermath of the Black Death. Higher wages and lower prices meant that more people could afford to eat meat, replace shoes, containers or harness, even use more tallow for candles. The butcher graziers that congregated around regional centres supplied this demand and in places came near to monopolising supplies to the leather trade. In late fourteenth-century Exeter a combination of butchers from within the town and from the surrounding countryside was responsible for 95 per cent of the sale of skins and hides.[33] It is, then, not surprising to find butchers among the leaders of many small-town societies. And in Scotland, where even the largest towns were relatively small, butchers had probably always been significant general merchants, as was the case with one Bridinus, a butcher from Banff who, in the 1340s, was supplying cloth and fur to the king.[34]

*Long-distance trade*

With cattle dealers we are moving away from local trade and towards long-distance trade. The commodities produced in the British Isles that were marketed over long distances were overwhelmingly raw materials. Of these wool was the most abundant and the most lucrative, but hides, grain, fish, tin and lead were also in demand, and their significance should not be underestimated for regional economies. The economy of twelfth-century Yarmouth was so harnessed to fish, that there fish acted as a form of currency; Exeter's prosperity was founded in its trade in fish and hides, as were the fortunes of west- and south-coast Irish towns by the fifteenth century.[35] The only, but extremely important, exception to this welter of unprocessed (or semi-processed) commodities was cloth, primarily English cloth. English cloth featured as a luxury export in the twelfth century, but more significantly cloth was produced for a mass market not only in England, but also in Scotland and Wales, to an increasing extent from the second half of the fourteenth century onwards. However, cloth manufacture notwithstanding, towns were primarily the channelers of trade, rather than being places that generated new products for more distant markets.

Within the British Isles long-distance trade was in part a response to specialisation enforced by geography. Tin, iron and to some extent building materials had to be transported to places where they were not available. The movement of commodities was constrained by the extent to which they could bear the cost of transport. Cattle, conveniently, could take themselves to market, though they might get a bit thin on the way and, for example, having had to walk from Wales, might need fattening up on the lush pastures outside Coventry or Warwick before being sold on. But the costs of carrying inanimate produce should not be overly exaggerated in lowland areas; grain could be moved up to 20 miles overland without the cost becoming prohibitive. By water it would cost less than half as much to move, and it should be noticed that this very significant price differential was one of the factors that could skew and extend the areas of influence of those market towns and 'higher order' regional centres on navigable rivers or beside the coast.[36]

Exports from the British Isles to other parts of Europe were also almost entirely of raw materials, with again the partial exception of cloth. In return all parts of the British Isles imported luxuries: wine, spices, dyes, fine cloths, furs. More mundane products that were also in short supply (or more conveniently brought in by sea) were also imported: iron, timber, salt. To this by the fifteenth century was added a rapidly increasing range of both cheap and sophisticated consumer goods, anything from saucepans and kettles to scissors and paper or drinking glasses and playing tables.[37]

Overseas trade was extremely important in shaping the pattern of town foundation and urban distribution. Most Irish trade was connected to the European network through English ports before the fifteenth century, so that the most successful Irish towns were to be found along the south and east coasts: Dublin, Waterford, Cork. Limerick and Galway only came into their own with the growth of direct trade between Ireland and the Mediterranean in the late fifteenth century. Scottish trade that was not directed towards England was almost entirely focused on northern Europe, with a triangular trade between Scotland, the Low Countries and the Baltic in the later middle ages. Hence, up until the late fifteenth century, Scottish towns were overwhelmingly founded along the eastern side of the country with the ports of Aberdeen, Perth, Dundee, Edinburgh and, until the fourteenth century, Berwick, as by far the most successful.

The importance of overseas trade was almost as graphically represented in the distribution of English towns up to the early fourteenth century, with some of the most spectacular successes among the new towns founded in the twelfth century being east-coast ports: Boston, King's Lynn, Yarmouth, Newcastle upon Tyne. These four, along with two other ports, London and Bristol, made up six of the ten wealthiest towns in the early fourteenth century.[38] But the emergence of England during the later middle ages as one of the 'nodal points of European trade', with an important role as an entrepôt for trade from the Baltic and north Germany, the Low Countries, Gascony, Spain and the Mediterranean, inevitably meant changes in the pattern of trade routes and the commodities handled.[39] One of the considerations of this chapter must therefore be how changes in long-distance trade affected the relative prosperity of English coastal towns.

Although in terms of overall value overseas trade was probably always less significant than the internal market, its impact on the way that the urban hierarchy was structured was very great. The place of any one town in the hierarchy was heavily influenced by the extent to which it acted as a point for collection and distribution of the commodities of long-distance trade. This means that there was not always a direct correlation between the size of a town and whether it can be ranked as a first- or second-order centre. The point can be illustrated by a comparison between Exeter and Southampton in the later middle ages, where a great deal is known about the distance to which each town's commercial tentacles extended. Exeter, in the late fourteenth century, had a population of c.3200, rather larger than that of Southampton at c.2100. But Exeter's sphere of influence was far narrower than that of Southampton. Seventy per cent of the shipping coming into Exeter in the late fourteenth and fifteenth centuries was coastal trade, and Exeter merchants were occupied in the redistribution of goods imported through other ports: Plymouth, Dartmouth or Southampton. The wine, dyes and iron that arrived in Exeter in this way were mostly sold at market towns within Devon.[40] In contrast, Southampton served a far wider market because it was the chief port used by Italian merchants, and so an entrepôt for luxuries such as silks, glass and spices as well as for the wine and dyes that were in constant demand. Southampton had commercial contacts in an area extending up to 80 miles around the port, with dyes being carried even further, over 100 miles to Coventry, on a regular basis.[41]

The change in the relative size and prosperity of these two towns by the late fifteenth and early sixteenth centuries were profound, illustrative of the realignment of the urban hierarchy caused in large measure by the decline in wool exports and the growth of the cloth industry. By the 1520s Southampton was still ahead of Exeter in terms of the value of its overseas trade, ranking second among provincial towns after Bristol. But its prosperity was fragile because it was so wholly dependent on the Italian merchants who controlled the import and export business, and whose profits were not invested in Southampton. Exeter had moved into a position of being the third most significant exporter among provincial towns on the strength of its cloth exports, drawing as it could on the textile output of the rapidly industrialising Devon hinterland. Exeter itself was part of the industrial boom and can be seen as bounding ahead of Southampton in both size and wealth. By 1524 it was twice as large as Southampton and paying four times as much in tax.

Much of the regulation of trade described earlier is indicative of the consciousness of medieval townsmen that they needed to work at defending their position as distributive centres. This was particularly the case for towns in out-of-the-way places, where constant intervention in the market might be necessary to attract trade. The practice of Scottish councils in the later middle ages of bulk buying cargoes may well have been to guarantee sales to alien ships tempted to go to other ports. Aberdeen made corporate purchases of grain and salt in the fifteenth century, and likewise at Wigtown in remote Galloway in 1525 the alderman and bailies bought the entire cargo of salt from a passing 'France man callit Geliane', paying for it in hides and cloth as well as cash.[42] It seems plausible that the surprising and temporary success of the small Scottish west-coast port of Kirkcudbright in the fifteenth century was the result of the enthusiastic support of the Douglas family.[43] Sometimes geography defeated a town's best efforts. The silting up of a harbour, as happened to Yarmouth, served to compound the problems that the town was having in the slump of the mid-fifteenth century, and resulted in a savage reduction of its fishing fleet.[44]

But Yarmouth's difficulties were not all down to geography; some arose as a result of human agency, significantly war and piracy. Crown policy and crown intervention in the passage of trade, made in order either to raise money or to frustrate the objectives of rival political powers, could have a fundamental impact on the patterns of trade and hence on the prosperity of towns, their future, or lack of future, as distributive centres. This was not just a case of violent fluctuations in the traffic going through any one port, as goods were made subject to arbitrary embargoes and confiscations, as privileges were rescinded or granted to rivals, though all these contributed to the habitual volatility of trade that medieval merchants had to accommodate – and which regularly gave rise to despairing petitions as to how they faced utter ruin. Crown intervention could also influence the long-term alignment of trade, as is most evident in the case of wool and cloth.

Wool was the most lucrative commodity in long-distance trade for much of the middle ages in England and Scotland, and for a while in those parts of Ireland where sheep, particularly monastic flocks, were introduced through the manorial economy. In the twelfth and thirteenth centuries the wool was destined largely for the industrial cities of Flanders and of northern Italy, where its quality made it very highly valued. It was the voracity of the demand for wool that made it possible for the Crown to raise revenue from the sale of wool and which resulted in policies that helped to drastically change the scale and orientation of the trade. The profitability of the wool trade made it the target of many conflicting interest groups, all of whom sought to maximise their share: denizen middlemen who bought from growers and sold to exporters, denizen and alien exporters, and of course the Crown itself; all had different agendas. Crown intervention manipulating these different interest groups both served to channel wool sales into the hands of an ever-decreasing number of urban merchants, and ultimately helped to switch the interest of entrepreneurs to the manufacture of cloth rather than the export of wool. In showing how this was worked out, the territories controlled by the English Crown will be considered first before turning to the way the Crown in Scotland handled overseas trade in wool.

Though towns did act as collection points for English and Welsh wool, there was initially no need for the wool trade to pass through any town until it reached a port of embarkation, and indeed much of the wool trade in the thirteenth century was conducted by direct negotiation between exporting merchants and producers or local woolmongers. The imposition of customs duties on overseas trade introduced during the thirteenth century makes it possible to identify the English ports benefiting from this trade, even if the passage of wool to those ports cannot be certain. They were virtually all on the east coast. Boston and then London headed the table in England, though London was moving ahead fast by the early fourteenth century, with a string of east-coast towns from Newcastle, through York and Hull to Lynn and Yarmouth handling most of the rest of the trade, and with Southampton as the only south-coast English port to figure as a significant exporter.

The desire of the Crown to increase customs revenues led it to impose regulations on which towns should be the foci of the wool trade. The device of establishing wool staples exemplifies the policy of channelling wool in order to tax it more effectively and also illustrates the conflicting interests of the various parties along the chain of supply. Staple towns were first nominated in the early fourteenth century, as the sole venues through which all wool had to pass for export. Throughout the fourteenth century, as different pressure groups gained the ascendancy, the staple passed from overseas, in Flanders and northern France, to a series of home staples in England, Wales and Ireland. If staples had to exist then home staples were favoured by middlemen, not themselves exporters, who found this gave them a wider range of customers and better prices than an overseas staple; conversely home staples irritated denizen exporting merchants unless they lived in or near one of the favoured towns such as London, York, Lincoln or Dublin.

The power of the exporting merchants proved ultimately to be the strongest and an overseas staple was finally established at Calais in 1363, controlled by the Company of the Staple, a small London-based group of merchants, and through which all but wools from Northumberland had in theory to pass. Because dealers in Irish wool found this monumentally inconvenient, the Irish parliament ruled in 1429 that the Calais staple did not apply to them. That this ruling was not tested in the courts until 1483 is evidence both of the insignificance of Irish wool exports by the fifteenth century and the lack of effective English interest in Irish affairs by that date.[45] Some exceptions to the staple policy were made, affecting elements of the English market; most significantly, Italians were allowed to export wool direct to the Mediterranean from Southampton, an exemption which, as will be seen, caused no end of grief to Londoners. For of course the advantage of the Calais staple lay mainly with those shipping through London, for whom the arrangements were most convenient. The result was that the export trade in wool from other east-coast ports began a decline from which it never recovered.

Although London was taking an ever-larger share of wool exports, the entire wool trade was contracting from the 1360s onwards. The establishment of the staples was only one aspect of the Crown's fiscal policies that served not only to redirect the path of trade but also to change its nature drastically. Particularly significant in this respect was the enormous increase in customs duties imposed by Edward III from 1336 onwards in order to fund his wars. Comprehensive customs duties on wool exports had been imposed for the first time in 1275 and were supplemented by additional levies, or by the requisitioning of wool en masse in various experiments to realise more money from the trade in wool. However it was the extreme measures taken by Edward III from 1336 onwards which had the most profound effect on this trade. The raising of the level of duty on exported wool meant that whereas cloth exports carried a duty of about 5 per cent of their value, wool was carrying duties of some 33 per cent of its value. Because the rise in duties proved permanent, the English cloth industry had a formidable and enduring competitive advantage, so that not only could home demand be satisfied from production, but cloth became increasingly significant as an export. Other factors served to reinforce the advantage of the domestic cloth industry. After the Black Death the drastic reduction of the rural population meant a move away from labour-intensive arable farming and towards livestock farming, particularly sheep farming. The result was the overproduction of wool, whose price collapsed in the 1380s, and remained low for the rest of the middle ages. This made the move into cloth production even more advantageous for the English at a time when the difficulties of their Flemish competitors were compounded by violent unrest and civil war. The tunnel vision of the remaining wool exporters enhanced the attraction of switching to cloth for many entrepreneurs. The determination of the Staplers to monopolise what was left of a declining trade eventually helped to kill the goose that laid the golden eggs. By the 1420s and 1430s cloth exports had overtaken wool exports in value, and having survived the doldrum years of the mid-fifteenth century, resumed their triumphant climb. Whereas in the mid-fourteenth century some 4000 cloths a year had been exported, by 1400 this was 40 000 and by 1500 around 80 000.[46]

More will be said later about the growth of the English cloth industry and the way that its expansion fuelled the growth of places which had previously been of minor significance. The point at issue here is how far cloth sales, whether for the home or the overseas market, were channelled through existing regional distribution centres. It depended not only on whether the regional centre itself became a major cloth manufacturer, but also on how far its merchants could control the marketing of cloth manufactured in the town's rural hinterland. The experience was mixed; some towns were significantly more successful than others, but equally the capacity of any one town to attract the cloth trade might vary considerably over the period 1350–1500. There were some outright losers. Boston, which had been the major provincial wool port in the thirteenth and early fourteenth centuries, had no place in the cloth trade. In Alan Dyer's league tables of urban wealth Boston had slithered far down, from third place in 1334 to twenty-second by the 1520s. Other towns had a temporary success. York was a major cloth manufacturing town in the late fourteenth century, exporting its cloth, and that of its hinterland, through Hull. But by the later fifteenth century it was losing out badly, its cloth industry contracting, the failure of its export drive evident in the dwindling amount of cloth taken out of Hull by Yorkshire merchants. In contrast to York, Norwich was a survivor, retaining its role as a manufacturer and distributor of cloth, and Exeter was a boom town, its growth fed by its expanding cloth industry and position as a cloth exporter.

In terms of exports the most significant losers were the towns in the north and east, the gainers being the towns in the south. It was a shift that was reinforced once again by the growing control that London exercised over the market. By 1500 it was accounting for roughly 60 per cent of all cloth exports, a figure that had risen to 80 per cent by the 1530s. The only other significant cloth-exporting towns by the late fifteenth century were those in the south that shipped a great deal of their cloth direct to the Mediterranean: Bristol, Exeter, Southampton. London's ascendancy was reinforced by the coalescence of London cloth merchants in the Company of Merchant Adventurers in the later fifteenth century. Not only did this powerful company bypass the merchants of provincial centres, for example buying direct from the cloth manufacturers of the West Riding to outflank the merchants of York and Hull, but their interests were also focused very narrowly on the market in the Low Countries. It is probably as a result of this that they showed little interest in defending the northern markets, those of the Baltic in particular, which were of key importance to the ports of the north-east.

Whereas crown interference can be seen to have been a major factor in restructuring the export trade in wool and cloth in England, a similar degree of intervention was not so evident in Scotland. Towns of regality were founded with special privileges, giving them a monopoly of exports; those so privileged were known as cocket towns, their licence symbolised by the cocket or stamp of customs officials. The intention was to funnel international trade through points where it could easily be taxed. In reality a handful of east-coast towns controlled the wool trade, with exports going through the staple, which was located in Bruges from the early fourteenth century until 1471. Exports in wool from Scotland also began to decline from the 1380s and collapsed in the fifteenth century. As in England, overproduction meant a fall in prices, demand from the Low Countries contracted and those towns which had been overdependent on the market in wool found themselves painfully exposed. For in Scotland the decline in wool exports was not compensated for by a rise in the export of cloth, and not until the 1520s did cloth become a significant commodity in Scottish overseas trade. Such overseas trade as was left was concentrated more and more in Edinburgh, which handled about 70 per cent of wool and cloth exports by the 1470s.[47] Scottish provincial towns were forced to restructure in various ways. Aberdeen concentrated on the export of salmon. Dundee turned to cloth manufacture, most of which must have gone to the home market – and this may have been the way of salvation for a number of other towns.

## Traders

As the previous section has suggested, everywhere commercial advantage could be bought in return for loans to the Crown, an issue that will be returned to later when considering the provision of financial services by the urban rich. But for the English Crown, whose financial needs always took priority over the long-term interests of denizen merchants, commercial privileges could just as readily be granted to rival interest groups, which brings us to the question of who was profiting from all this long-distance trade.

A substantial amount of overseas trade was undertaken by aliens, and their participation had some bearing on which towns were able to profit most from long-distance trade, both inland and overseas. Up until the thirteenth century it was probably alien merchants who controlled most of the overseas trade of the British Isles. It is presumed that this was the case for Scotland, where both Flemings and Italians were in evidence in the thirteenth century, and it was only after the Wars of Independence that native merchants took over. It is less certainly the case for Ireland; although there were Italian merchants there, functioning as tax collectors as well as shippers, but they had disappeared by the early fourteenth century.[48] The evidence is much more abundant for England, where the favoured position of first Flemings up till 1270, and then Gascons and Italians, was a matter of crown policy. It was these merchants who could most readily be tapped to fund the ambitions of the English Crown, a consideration that became even more crucial with the vastly expanded war aims of Edward I. The wool ports of the east coast, conveniently near the major international fairs, best served the interests of the Flemings; Southampton was the favoured port of the Italians.

The financial expedients of the English Crown were one of the factors that contributed to the shift of overseas trade away from alien merchants and into the hands of denizens, for the Crown's financial interests were ultimately best served by fixing monopolies in wool on a group of indigenous merchants, rather than by promoting aliens. But even after English merchants had established their ascendancy, alien merchants still retained a significant share both of imports and exports. They came to take a substantial share of the expanding cloth export business, and privileges granted to them could still be used as a stick with which to beat indigenous merchants if the latter proved recalcitrant over crown demands. Two groups of aliens were particularly privileged: merchants from the Baltic and north Germany, associated in the Hanse, a confederation of towns that negotiated joint privileges for their members, and merchants from Italy.

The merchants of the Hanse were in fact exceptionally privileged, to the extent that they had some taxation advantages over even denizen merchants. Whilst these privileges constituted no real threat to English enterprise, the Hanse was not generally resented. Indeed, in the fifteenth century, the merchants of Bristol, when they traded through London, were inclined to be more favourably disposed to Hanse merchants than they were to Londoners, for the former paid hard cash, rather than making payment in 'Cardes, tenys balles, fish hooks, bristills, tassells and such other simple wars', which the Bristol men scathingly accused the Londoners of doing.[49] Where Hanse merchants did cause grief was in towns on the east coast during the fifteenth century as they gradually succeeded in shutting the Baltic to English merchants trading in cloth; this was a particular blow for northern merchants already contending with the fact that a growing proportion of overseas trade went via London.

Far more generally disliked than the German merchants were the Italians. Londoners had a particularly tense relationship with Italian merchants because privileges granted to the Italians by the Crown threatened London's position as an entrepôt. The busy trade of Southampton in the later middle ages rode on the back of exemptions granted to Italian merchants that enabled them to sail with English goods straight to the Mediterranean and bring back to Southampton, and not to London, the wines, dyestuffs and spices that were so valuable to the distributive trade of inland merchants. The specific interests of alien merchants meant that they were far more of a presence in some ports than in others. Bristol was never a wool port and that in part accounts for the fact that where Southampton was heaving with Italians, the trade of Bristol was almost entirely in English hands.

Whereas alien merchants maintained a significant presence in England in the fourteenth and fifteenth centuries they seem largely to have disappeared from Scotland. Their trade had been valued and solicited: Wallace wrote to the cities of Hamburg and Lübeck in 1297 specifically inviting Hanseatic traders back to the country, and during the Wars of Independence German merchants supplied Scotland with arms and foodstuffs from the Low Countries.[50] But it was the period of the Wars of Independence which saw the shift towards the control of Scotland's overseas trade by Scottish merchants, though the process by which this occurred cannot be traced in the same way as can be done for England.

The word 'merchant' when applied to denizens embraced a very wide variety of people, not just the international merchant operating in several countries, but anyone down to the small-scale, local dealer. The term 'merchant' was not in fact widely used until the later middle ages, when it came to be applied to one occupied in wholesale trade, but it still remained imprecise in its application. However, two general points apply to most of those who can be described as merchants and who were involved in long-distance trade: they were men, not women, and they did not specialise in one commodity to the exclusion of all others.

It was certainly possible for women to be occupied in trade. The legal status of *femme sole* was held to apply to married women wanting to trade on their own account, and whose husbands could not be held liable for their debts. Additionally, widows were specifically granted the right to continue in their husbands' businesses. But in reality women are very seldom found among the big operators, in contrast to their extensive involvement in local trade. Alice Chester, living in Bristol in the fifteenth century, was one of the rare women found active in overseas trade, importing iron and exporting cloth. But tellingly, not only was she the widow of an important merchant, she also continued in business with the help of her son.[51] Women had no authority in public and political life, a point that will be returned to in Chapter 4; they were thus profoundly disadvantaged in the associations of merchants which negotiated and regulated the terms of long-distance trade. A successful woman trading long distance was almost always carrying on the business of a deceased husband, using the commercial networks that he had built up.

The second general point is that most merchants were not specialists. Some specialist middlemen did emerge; the cornmongers are an early example, appearing in London in the early fourteenth century, controlling the very considerable grain trade needed to victual the city. London was unusual among English towns in that merchants were grouped in guilds or companies that were, on the face of it, identified with a particular commodity: fishmongers, grocers, vintners, drapers. These merchants might have retail outlets but their money was in wholesaling, and within each guild or company there was a clear distinction between the minority mercantile element, marked out publicly by a distinct livery, and the artisanal majority. There was a tendency among the merchants to gravitate towards dealing in particular commodities, in line with the prevailing interest of the city company to which they belonged, for example in late medieval London mercers concentrated on cloth, grocers on spices and dyes. But if they were freemen of London there was in fact no bar to them trading in whatever they wished, and merchants were more typically very versatile in the commodities that they handled and opportunistic in their operations. John Chigwell, a member of the Fishmongers Company in the early fourteenth century, far from sticking to fish, in the course of one complex transaction dealt with woad from Picardy and carried beans, wine and salt from London to Scotland and wool and hides back from Scotland to St Omer.[52] Nor did merchants restrict themselves to trade. The fabulously wealthy Canynges family of late medieval Bristol, for example, expanded and diversified their operations as new opportunities arose. They were cloth entrepreneurs as well as merchants, subsequently branching out into shipowning and shipbuilding, with William Canynges the Younger reputedly employing 800 men in his ships and another 100 making or repairing them.[53]

Given both the relative lateness of the use of the term 'merchant', the lack of specialisation and the attractions of long-distance trade to the aspiring artisan, it is not surprising to find that wholesale and long-distance trade was at all times, and in nearly all places, handled by people who identified themselves by a craft ascription. This was commoner in small towns, but the circumstances of urban growth meant this also might apply in larger towns that acted as regional centres. The cappers, on the strength of a manufacturing speciality, became one of the leading mercantile groups in Coventry in the late fifteenth and early sixteenth centuries.[54] In some of the largest Scottish towns the term 'merchant' was relatively uncommon even in the fifteenth century, with long-distance trade being controlled by an elite within the crafts, as was the case in Perth and Edinburgh.

Other less general observations can be made about the people who were occupied in long-distance trade, and which relate more specifically to different regions of the British Isles or to different sizes of town. Merchants moved up from smaller to larger towns as their ambitions expanded. This became necessary as merchants from larger towns moved in to take a significant share of the trade of small towns; where a hierarchy of towns began to emerge this tendency can be seen operating at each level. So, for example, the burgesses of Stratford-upon-Avon were commercially dependent on merchants from Coventry, Worcester and Bristol.[55] Bristol, as a major regional centre, spread its tentacles very wide. Its merchants entered into partnership with men from Wells, had agents in Shrewsbury and dealings in Cardiff. Not surprisingly, they can be found holding property in Irish towns and leasing salmon fisheries on the west coast of Ireland, so that it was popularly said that 'heryng of Slegoy (Sligo) and salmon of bame (Bann) heis made in brystowe mony a riche man'. Men from Coventry and Chester also had an active interest in the Irish trade as well, concentrating their attentions on Dublin, whereas the Bristol merchants focused on the south-coast towns. The guild for visiting merchants established in Dublin in the late fifteenth century was suspected by the Dubliners as being a ruse whereby the English could get a firmer control on Irish trade.[56]

Individuals or partnerships might be operating out of provincial towns on a great many fronts, as did William Doncaster of Chester, who marketed lead from Wales, wine from Gascony and grain from Ireland and who exported wool through Ipswich in the early fourteenth century.[57] But the scope for English provincial merchants, particularly in the crucial wool trade, was ultimately narrowed as a result of the Crown's fiscal policies. As already discussed, the various experiments made on the taxation of wool had shown that crown interests were best served by fixing monopolies on a group of indigenous merchants from whom often huge financial advances could be demanded. Initially among the beneficiaries of these monopolies were the big provincial merchants, and in fact the most formidable syndicate in the 1340s was headed by a group of northern merchants based in York and Hull. The sheer scale of the wool trade, the extent of crown demands and hence the profitability of the privileges that could be acquired meant that one northern wool merchant, William de la Pole of Hull, was able to buy the family into the peerage as Earls of Suffolk. Men like Pole had become more than merchants, they were crown financiers, 'virtually commercial civil servants'. A privileged group of some forty merchants in this category were separated off from the majority of those involved in long-distance trade.[58]

However, the narrowing of interest went further; the long-term effect of crown policy was to concentrate mercantile capital more and more in London. As London became the focus of an ever-larger percentage of overseas trade, with the wool and cloth trades increasingly monopolised by the Staplers and Merchant Adventurers, so London merchants became the most important source of crown finance in England. Merchants from

provincial towns needed to form partnerships with Londoners, join
London companies and send family members to set up in London if they
wanted to be serious players in overseas trade. Londoners in turn placed
agents in provincial towns where there was a potential commercial
threat, and in Southampton they became mixed up in local politics in
order to try and neutralise what was seen as the malign crown preference for Italians.[59]

One of the spin-offs of commercial centralisation, and particularly of
the concentration of the cloth trade in London, was the emergence of
a new breed of dealer. Chapmen, aggressively upwardly mobile from
the mid-fifteenth century onwards, brought cloth to London from the
provinces and there stocked up on the consumer goods that were in increasing demand back home, thereby effectively cutting out provincial
wholesalers.[60] The inventory of Thomas Gryssop, a York chapman,
made as early as 1446 shows painfully how the trend was going. His
debts indicate that many of his goods were now obtained not from his
own home city, still a major centre of overseas trade, but instead were
purchased in London. What Gryssop's inventory also illustrates is the
sheer range of relatively inexpensive goods available by this date, bringing if not exactly sophistication, at least a touch of style to potential
customers in rural Yorkshire. Among his wares Gryssop had dozens of
different types of leather goods, 'trewlufe purses' at $1\frac{1}{2}d$ each, swans-
weng purses at $5d$ and leather gloves, black gloves and furred gloves for
men and for women. He also had caps and bonnets for adults and children, silk ribbons and mirrors, and sugar, cinnamon and green ginger
to spice up their lives.[61]

## Manufacturing

What is striking about the range of goods available to the fifteenth-
century consumer is how many of them were imported. So just what was
being made in towns in the British Isles, and how can urban industry be
characterised? It is easier to get a sense of the range of occupations than
of the overall occupational structure of any one town. Although up to
the mid-fourteenth century some people identified themselves by a
particular skill or speciality, the majority did not. It was only with the
increase in labour legislation after the Black Death that it was made a
statutory requirement for everyone to make themselves known by the
craft from which they derived the major portion of their income.[62] As

already discussed, this tidy approach disguised the way in which the multi-occupational household worked, and probably served in particular to misrepresent the number of people who derived some of their income from the food industry. However, broadly speaking, apart from food and drink, the staples of urban production were consumer basics, leatherware and textiles, with ironwork and some non-ferrous metals. Where documentary evidence is lacking, archaeology has confirmed a similar kind of spread. Excavations in Perth have produced evidence of extensive leatherworking, and of the manufacture of cheap cloth, of the debris from smithies and, so far, only one workshop dedicated to non-ferrous metals. Equally, in the considerably larger town of Dublin, archaeologists have turned up much evidence of leatherworking and weaving, with additionally quantities of boneworking. In Dublin and Perth pottery making was also still a 'great mass production industry', either within the town or in the suburbs in the thirteenth century, whereas it had largely migrated to the countryside in England by the late twelfth century.[63]

The particular nature of a settlement might allow for the occasional more exotic expertise to flourish even in a small town. In twelfth-century Evesham there was, as well as a weaver, fullers, carpenters and smiths, a parchmentmaker, whose chief market must have been the monks of Evesham Abbey, the town's lord. Likewise, twelfth-century Battle, again by the gates of an abbey, boasted a goldsmith and a bellfounder, as well as the victuallers, clothmakers and leatherworkers that one would expect to find.[64] However, as a general rule, small towns could not hope for the kind of sustained demand that would support artisans dedicated to the making and repairing of silver items or casting bells. And indeed, the record of Battle Abbey's purchasing in the fourteenth and fifteenth centuries shows the monks turning their backs on their own town, going rather to Hastings, Canterbury or London for much of their shopping.[65] In small towns the single representative of a craft, for example the resident brazier, working in non-ferrous metals, would turn his hand to what his customers required of him to the limit of his ability, but would perforce present his customers with a limited range. Only in a regional centre would there be a large enough market for artisans to specialise. So, for example, in late medieval York there were bellmakers, potters (making large bronze vessels and small bells), founders who made kitchenware, lattoners making small memorial items and memorial brasses and lorimers casting the metal parts of harness. And it was the larger town, the regional centres, which by the later middle ages can be shown to be satisfying the demand for luxury goods from the wealthy and status-conscious purchaser, with London offering the most dazzling array of all. To a very limited extent there were regional manufacturing specialisms. Whereas the cloth industry was ubiquitous, certain towns on the eastern side of England, particularly Stamford and Lincoln, had a reputation in the twelfth century for producing cloth of exceptionally high quality. In the later middle ages the massive expansion of the cloth industry increased the variety of cloths in production and led to new centres of specialised manufacture; fourteenth-century Colchester, for example, concentrated on russets, a practical, decently made but not exciting fabric much used by the religious orders.[66] Rising standards of living in the later middle ages meant that other commodities were beginning to find a mass market, and in this market certain local lines gathered a growing reputation for quality. The Coventry cappers flourished on the strength of what was, on the face of it, fairly ordinary knitted headgear; the chapman Thomas Gryssop had Doncaster knives in his chapman's pack; Nottingham artisans, responding to the formidable increase on pious spending by the late medieval laity, had a notable reputation for alabaster carvings of religious subjects. But, as already pointed out, much of the new market was satisfied from the shiploads of miscellaneous goods brought in from continental Europe. Despite the examples given above of regional specialisation, there was no real broadening of the industrial base of British towns. Ultimately the characteristic product of the urban workshop within the British Isles was neither a sumptuous fabric or a silver spoon, but the humble shoe.

The first question to address is, who was employed in urban industry – was there a gender bias to certain kinds of work? Women can be found in both skilled and unskilled employment in virtually all kinds of job, but this does not necessarily mean that they were habitually so employed, or that they could hope to be paid on an equal basis with men. Women might be commandeered to even very heavy unskilled work in an emergency. Edward I, in extreme haste to strengthen his castles at Linlithgow and Dumfries in his 1302 campaign against Scotland, drafted in women ditchers in very considerable numbers, paying them $1\frac{1}{2}d$ a day compared to the $2d$ earned by male ditchers.[67] The appearance of these women is unusual in the context of royal building accounts, but the possibility is raised that they might have been employed as site clearers or rubble carriers whenever there was a local shortage of labour.

Women were equally accepted as skilled labour in some of the heavier manufacturing industries. A craftsman's wife was recognised as a key part of the workforce in the York founder's ordinances, which allowed an artisan to take on an extra apprentice if he had no wife to assist him. Adam Hecche, a York armourer, split his business between the 'craft of fourbourcraft', that is, the making of plate armour, which went to his son John, and the making of chain mail that went to his daughter Agnes.[68] But the way Hecche made his split is in fact symptomatic of the overall orientation of male and female occupations. Women do not turn up with any frequency in occupations that demanded great physical strength, such as tanning or working as smiths. Rather, women's work tended to concentrate on those skills that were an extension of household tasks: needlework and knitting, the various stages of textile manufacture, victualling. They often took work which could be done part-time and would fit in with their other obligations, and which might complement the work of the head of the household: Matthew Roberd was a wiredrawer in Bury St Edmunds in the fourteenth century; his daughter Margaret worked as a cardmaker, fitting wire hooks into leather backs to make the cards needed for preparing wool.[69]

Women, if single, were also less secure than men in what was always a volatile employment market, and when work became short, the presumption was that men should have preference over women in taking what work was available. Characteristic was the agitation against the Bristol weavers who 'occupien and hiren ther wyfes, doughtours and maidens, some to weve in ther owne lombes and some to hire them to wirche with othour persons of the seid Crafte'.[70] This agitation had been prompted by a contraction in the cloth industry that threatened male employment. Historians now suggest that it was the late fourteenth and early fifteenth centuries that had offered the most opportunities to women for independent employment, because of labour shortages, but as always this generalisation has to be related to the economic fortunes of specific towns.

The involvement of women as skilled labour in a wide variety of jobs has implications for our understanding of the way the workforce was trained and for the significance of the system of apprenticeship. Women were trained to a high degree of skill almost always without formal apprenticeship. The only real exception to this were the London silk-women of the later middle ages, whose craft was unique in being controlled by wealthy women.[71] In most occupations, girls learnt their skills in their own homes. The same was probably true of a great many boys.

Apprenticeship meant the attachment of a young person to another household for training, not only as a means of inculcating skills but also to advance expectations, buying access to a more prestigious occupation. It tends to be associated with the system of craft guilds, but could and did just as easily operate independently of the crafts. When apprenticeship was integrated into the formal organisation of crafts it carried a social as well as an economic significance, slotting the apprentice into a fixed place in the social hierarchy and marking out those supposedly at the first stage of the occupational ladder. The objective was to climb high enough up the ladder to become an independent master, but for a great many, and in some industries for the majority of young hopefuls, there was in reality a fairly high chance of never moving off the bottom rungs, but rather spending a life dependent on piece work. And this brings us to the matter of how urban industry was organised.

*Industrial organisation*

Urban industry was almost entirely domestic. The basic unit comprised the artisan and his wife, with possibly the assistance of a servant or apprentice, making and selling goods from the same site. The technology available did not warrant factory production; the household unit was perfectly adequate, and what is particularly striking about urban industry is the smallness of its scale and the limited extent of investment in fixed capital. The largest outfit recorded in late medieval London, that of a pewterer, employed 18 people, but this was exceptional, and it was far more usual to find, even among wealthy households, no more than one or two servants.

A few industries required fairly extensive specialised plant. John Yowdale, a Durham tanner, had a major investment of 16 lead cisterns in his tenement which was, equally importantly, well supplied with water.[72] Breweries and foundries needed furnaces, but furnaces were used in a number of processes and a workshop could easily be adapted to the needs of new tenant. This can make it difficult for archaeologists to pin down exactly what was going on in any one site, but it does underline the essential simplicity of many industrial premises. The inventories of artisans, which begin to survive from the later middle ages, also give an indication of how limited investment in tools might be. William Thwaite, a York founder who died in 1512, very comfortably off with assets of over £36 in all, had equipment consisting of patterns, files, hammers and a mould worth under £3.[73] For a weaver, the complex horizontal loom (which had been introduced into England by the twelfth century) could cost 30–40s by the fifteenth century; however there were still cheap vertical looms in use in Scotland in the later middle ages which would have involved much less outlay. And the equipment of a cobbler or a bowstringmaker would be even less, amounting to no more than a few shillings in value. To put these figures into context, a skilled artisan on a wage could expect to earn up to £7 a year by the fifteenth century, so the cost of setting up in business was not prohibitively high. Materials were much more expensive to stockpile; Thwaite's supplies of metal were worth about £8–£9. The cost of having so much capital tied up in stock might be the most crucial determinant against an artisan becoming an independent operator, making it necessary for him or her to undertake piecework. Here the image of the master craftsman, head of a household dedicated to the manufacture and sale of goods, begins to come a bit unstuck. The extent to which manufacture was done either on the basis of piece work or as wage labour depended on the industry involved. Although the amount of work performed in this way cannot be quantified it would be unwise to underestimate it. There is, however, the proviso that the surviving evidence, coming as it does from larger towns and from the later middle ages, gives prominence to this form of work and that in small towns it may have been less prevalent.

But there was one industry which everywhere was dependent on wage labour, and that was the building industry. There was some contract work for master carpenters, tilers or masons in the building or renovation of houses. A few entrepreneurs even emerged from amongst building workers as a result of their engagement on lucrative or highly prestigious projects. Occasionally, like Henry Yevele, king's mason in the fourteenth century, they were spectacularly successful.[74] But major building contracts might equally go to merchants who were in a good position to requisition materials, as was the case with the contracts for repairs to Edinburgh castle in the 1330s.[75] And most urban building workers found themselves employed not on constructing new buildings, but making alterations and repairs to existing houses, walls and pavements. If they were lucky they might become a regular employee of one of the major institutional landowners within a town, for example repairing guild property or troubleshooting for the council, but it was still work done on a daily basis for skilled and unskilled alike.

Among the manufacturing crafts, some industries lent themselves particularly to the employment of wage labour, usually in the form of piece work. Garment makers, for instance, customarily put out work to seamstresses – and did not necessarily pay very promptly. One can only hope that not all employees were as dismally served as Alys Legh, who worked as an embroiderer for the York vestmentmaker, Robert Locksmith; by the time he died in 1531, Locksmith owed her the substantial sum of 26s 8d for 'feyne hemynge of broderye'.[76] Bulk orders for military clothing or for charitable bequests of gowns for the poor must have galvanised a formidable number of needles into action.

The larger the demand for any one product, the more likely that it would be that the various stages of production would be split up and put out as piece work. Certainly a product might be made entirely in one household, but specialisation between different stages of manufacture emerged early on and increased as demand expanded enough to sustain the division of labour. The provision of shoes, an essential but not very durable product, illustrates the point. In the manufacture of leather goods, hides had to be tanned and then curried to make them supple before they could be worked up into different products. It was possible for one person to perform all these tasks, but more common to find them divided up. Shoemakers bought leather from tanners and then sent it out to a currier. Curriers seldom owned the leather they worked but were paid piece rates, differentiated according to whether the leather was being prepared for girdles, hose or shoes and according to the specific processes adopted for curing. Once curried, the leather went back to the shoemaker and was then put out again, this time to the shoemaker's servants to be made up. But the regulations drawn up by York city council in the early fifteenth century, relating to the contentious subject of how much shoemakers' servants should be paid, imply that the subdivision of labour could go even further. Some of the piece rates specified apply to the making of a whole boot or shoe. Others detailed payments such as 4d for sewing twelve pairs of shoes, $3\frac{1}{2}d$ for cutting twelve pairs of shoes and 1d for fitting a dozen soles.[77] Although shoemakers were generally amongst the poorest artisans, a canny and well-placed entrepreneur could build up a formidable business by dealing in leather and putting out work, and presumably this contributed to the way in which John Hammond, cobbler of Dublin, came to put together such a comfortable fortune in the late fourteenth century. The attenders at his lavish funeral were perhaps borne up by the comfort of Hammond shoes keeping their feet dry.[78]

Putting out work served the purposes of the entrepreneur who owned the materials out of which a product was manufactured and who could refuse to pay his outworkers if those materials were damaged or badly processed whilst in the outworkers' hands. The entrepreneur might also own the tools of the trade which he hired out, looms, for example, or even spinning wheels; the wife of Richard Taillour, a poor Colchester townsman, only surfaces in the records because she owed 10d for the lease of a spinning wheel.[79] It was in fact the textile industry which provided the most scope for entrepreneurs and which best exemplifies the subdivision of processes and the extent to which work was put out at piece rates. It should first be said that for all the great amount of information on the medieval textile industry there is still a great deal that is unknown. The Irish industry is almost completely uncharted; this means we have little knowledge of the manufacture of the internationally known mantles, heavy-duty outer garments that were made for export as well as for home consumption in Ireland.

Little is known either about the way that cheap cloth was produced for the domestic market. Much of it was probably made on narrow looms and left unfinished and undyed. It was very probably produced on a part-time basis, the secondary occupation of a household whose primary income was from another source. Hence the extent and distribution of cloth manufacture cannot be fully known, though certainly it was a great deal more extensive in the twelfth and thirteenth centuries than surviving records imply. Cheap cloth was made everywhere, and its manufacture seems to have been the staple of the Scottish cloth industry, a little of which found its way on to the export market, so that by the early fifteenth century in the Low Countries it was Scottish and Irish cloth 'of little value ... by which the poor and miserable folk are principally clothed'.[80]

It is not possible to equate the production methods adopted for these cheaper cloths with the organisation of the best known and documented aspect of the textile industry, the production of English broadcloths. This latter was an industry that was intensely regulated because of its growing importance in the export market; both the resulting amount of documentation on the industry, and the scale of investment it attracted, make it in some respects unique, but also make it possible to demonstrate fairly clearly the evolution of the subdivision of labour under the impetus of mass production.

Within the cloth industry the preparation of yarn was almost always done on a piece-work basis, usually by women, who washed, combed or carded, and spun the wool. The stages of cloth manufacture were divided between weavers, fullers who thickened the cloth and closed up the traces of the weave, shearmen who cropped and finished the cloth and the dyers. Any one of these artisans might be the person who organised the preparation of wool and orchestrated the manufacture of cloth. Alternatively the organisation might be in the hands of bigger fish: merchants or drapers. Just who the entrepreneurs were raises the question of how the textile industry was capitalised, not only within towns but also in the countryside, and this leads to the further issue of the extent to which rural industry was a threat to manufacturing in towns.

Weaving had always been an occupation practised in the countryside as well as the towns. The cloth industry of the twelfth and thirteenth centuries in England employed a considerable amount of rural labour, funded by urban entrepreneurs who might deliberately have used their rural employees to undermine the position of urban artisans. For the late twelfth and thirteenth centuries saw the creation of weavers' guilds within towns, guilds which generally unsuccessfully tried to guarantee the independence of artisans from their suppliers. The dismal and debt-ridden history of these guilds in the thirteenth century is indicative of their failure and of the extent to which the profits of cloth making had slipped from their hands, to be lodged firmly with the merchants, who controlled both production and the terms on which urban artisans were given employment. Competition from good-quality imports during the thirteenth century served to further underscore the precarious position of urban cloth workers.

From a position of some difficulty in the thirteenth century, English cloth manufacture expanded vastly in the fourteenth and fifteenth centuries, though not in a smooth and inexorably upward curve. Clothmaking also took off in parts of Wales, in the wake of English success. With the expansion of urban clothmaking in the fourteenth century, guilds of urban clothworkers once again emerged, taking part in the textile boom. But these guilds had little of the independence of action that the twelfth-century guilds had aspired to; they were different creatures, tolerated by the leading townsmen because they served a useful purpose in the regulation of the industry and constituted no threat to those in power.[81]

Individual artisans from among the clothworker crafts did prosper from this expansion, though different crafts acquired prominence in different towns. In fifteenth-century Ruthin a shearman, John 'fryseour', can be found leasing a fulling mill and dyeing cloth, controlling all stages of the finishing process.[82] The fullers were among the most successful clothworkers in fourteenth-century Colchester, acting as small-scale entrepreneurs, whereas in York, fullers were at the bottom of the pile. Weavers might be putting work out themselves and the prominence of weavers in Scottish towns in the later middle ages would suggest they had a significant part in cloth production. In late medieval England it seems that weavers increasingly had to work partly for themselves and partly as wage labourers making up other people's cloth; the poorest worked entirely as wage labourers. In his study of Colchester Britnell has emphasised the importance of the involvement of small producers, entrepreneurial artisans, in the cloth market, seeing them as chiefly responsible for Colchester's industrial growth in the later fourteenth century. At this stage investment by merchants and drapers was concentrated in the distribution of cloth. In this respect Britnell describes the industrial organisation in Colchester as 'primeval' compared to the huge enterprises of Flemish cloth entrepreneurs.[83] But the fifteenth century saw a growing concentration of textile manufacture in the hands of bigger operators, men calling themselves clothmakers, with artisans increasingly dependent on wage labour. And it was often the big entrepreneurs who controlled cloth production in the new centres of manufacture such as Lavenham.

New centres of manufacture emerged as the result of the growth of rural cloth production in the later middle ages, most notably in the West Riding of Yorkshire, East Anglia, Somerset and Devon. Whilst rural industry was booming, some towns failed entirely to cash in on the increased demand for cloth. Oxford, which had been an important centre for textile manufacture in the thirteenth century, never had any part in the late medieval expansion. Other towns such as York flourished for a while as cloth manufacturing centres, but failed to cope adequately with competition in the fifteenth century. In contrast, Norwich and Exeter prospered in what seems to have been a symbiotic relationship with rural industry. And complete newcomers such as Lavenham and Taunton showed formidable growth, in wealth derived from cloth production as much as in population.

As yet there is no wholly satisfactory way of explaining either the distribution of cloth production or the very different capacity of towns to sustain their own industries or to capitalise on the rural industry within their vicinity. However it is probably misleading to suggest that there was necessarily an outright rivalry, or a polarisation, between rural and urban industry, though this was the painfully felt experience of weavers in those towns where the textile industry was contracting. There is obvious evidence of competition, but this does not mean that rural industry was organised with no reference to towns, or that towns were somehow inimical to the manufacture of cloth by the fifteenth century. Newly wealthy places like Lavenham, Hadleigh and Taunton were all towns, not villages. Nor is there any reason to think that just because they were small towns, without an elaborate guild structure, these places could attract industry in the way that older established places with more complex institutions could not. The craft guilds of the large towns were in no position to drive up production costs by restrictive practices; they simply did not have that kind of power. And after all, not every large town did lose its cloth industry, though they may have experienced periodic difficulties in the course of the fifteenth century.

Rather than focusing on the relative cost advantage of rural or urban production, it seems more fruitful to think about successful towns as profiting in conjunction with the economic growth of their hinterlands. As already discussed, marketing networks changed in the later middle ages, with cloth-exporting merchants concentrated in a few southern ports. Provincial towns that were going to prosper were those that set up the most convenient networks linking the cloth entrepreneurs and the exporters. But the entrepreneurs themselves were changing. It was no longer just urban capital going into the manufacture of cloth. Enterprising landlords became involved in investment on their estates, for example the Mowbray enthusiasm for cloth production in Swansea was characteristic of the interest of marcher lords in manufacture.[84] But probably more significant for the growth of rural industry was the amount of capital being accumulated and invested by small-scale entrepreneurs among the yeoman farmers who emerged during the later middle ages. By the early sixteenth century these yeomen can be seen to have been extensively involved in the rural cloth industry, drawing on the resources of their families to extend their operations.[85] In the new nexus of rural clothier and London, Bristol or Exeter merchant, the old centres of distribution might prove irrelevant: Shrewsbury deserted for Welshpool or Oswestry as the Welsh clothiers found more convenient outlets closer to home.

*Quality control*

The sheer value of the export market meant that quality control became an ever-more prominent aspect of cloth manufacture during the course of the middle ages; a reputation for reliability needed to be maintained. Regulations had been set out in England as early as 1278 stipulating the size of broadcloths; subsequent legislation reiterated these dimensions and added specifications for other types of cloth as the market expanded. But quality control was also applied to more humble goods, produced for domestic consumption. As with the controls discussed earlier that were put into place over trade, this was largely a matter of consumer protection. The earliest recorded assize of bread dates back to the late twelfth century and a concern with the proper provision of food characterises much of the legislation, both national and local, throughout the period.

But by the fifteenth century inspection of standards had been extended way beyond foodstuffs, and urban authorities by that date might check on virtually any kind of product. One of the reasons that the subdivision of labour was not only encouraged, but also demanded by urban authorities, was that better scrutiny could be made of certain products if their manufacture was not entirely in the hands of one artisan. For example, by the fourteenth century strenuous efforts were being made to keep the two occupations of tanner and shoemaker distinct, at least in England (it seems likely that in Scotland the overlap between the two crafts remained). There was enough difficulty ensuring that leather goods such as shoes were adequate, without compounding the problem by letting tanners sneak sub-standard and illegal leathers into articles of their own manufacture. The fact that Walter Hyndwell, tanner in the small town of Thornbury, was fined for putting dead dogs in the river in the 1340s is probably a pointer to the ingenuity of this particular artisan, for Hyndwell was an illegal shoemaker as well as a tanner.[86] Whereas the assize of staple products such as bread and ale was always kept firmly in the hands of urban officials, by the fifteenth century quality control for manufactured goods was devolved wherever possible on to the members of the craft involved in production. Where a craft was formally constituted into a guild, the searchers of the craft were the officials responsible for maintaining standards, and were therefore the guild officials in which the town council took the most pressing interest. For there was more to quality control by this time than consumer protection. The elaboration of a system of craft guilds with their officials drafted in as agents of civic administration was, as will be seen in Chapter 3, a way of policing the workforce as well as of checking on standards of production.

### Service Industry

Although most of the information we have about industry in medieval towns relates to manufacturing, the service sector provided a primary or secondary income for a very large number of people. 'Service industry' provides an umbrella term under which nestle together an assortment of people in somewhat uneasy company, ranging from the academic and professional, for example lawyers in common or canon law, to services with a definite whiff of the unsalubrious, moral or physical: prostitution or the clearing of cesspits.

The unskilled, some of whom have already been briefly encountered as labourers in the building trades, were a great deal more numerous in the provision of services than were the professionals, but these unskilled were not the sort of people who were likely to appear in either burgess or tax records, so in any occupational profiles of a town based on written records they are likely to make an insignificant showing. The services these people offered pushed them to the margins of society. For women this might mean employment as laundresses or prostitutes. Although there were illegal professional brothels, run by females as well as males, that trapped the ignorant into prostitution, there were other women who sold their bodies only when all other forms of income dried up, and who moved in and out of prostitution. It was an ill-rewarded occupation, worth only 1*d* or 2*d* a night in the later middle ages, at a time when unskilled labour generally commanded 4*d* a day. Prostitution, strictly speaking, was not an occupational category. Contemporaries did not see it in economic terms; they made no distinction in theory between the whore with a reputation for promiscuity and the prostitute who needed to make money. But in practice certain kinds of lax sexual practice were acceptable. On its own the sheer number of clergy in medieval towns meant that there would always be a demand for unofficial semi-permanent arrangements. Isabella Wakefield of York sustained a long-term relationship with a local priest between 1402 and 1431; she had no difficulty finding testimonials for good character when she appeared before the courts. In contrast Margery Gray 'odirwys callyd Cherylipps', who also lived in York, was driven from parish to parish, and finally told to leave the city altogether because she attracted so many 'ill dispossid men . . . to the newsaunce of the neghbburs'.[87]

Ideologically at the opposite end of the spectrum to prostitutes, though in reality, as seen, at times rather more closely associated with them, were the clergy. In terms of its impact on the urban economy, probably one of the most seriously neglected of medieval service industries was the Church. This is not just a matter of the importance of the Church as a consumer of manufactured goods, though it was a large enough player in this field, but the Church as a provider of services that people wanted to pay for. Various factors led to the concentration of these services in towns. An urban church might become an important pilgrimage centre. Towns attracted the foundations of religious orders, especially friars, whose mendicant lifestyle depended on them being located near a constant source of alms. But the primary factor in concentrating clergy in towns was the financial and spiritual investment of the laity.

Late medieval Catholicism can be characterised as a demand-led religion; the laity sought the assurance of salvation in the multiplication of good works, and the most efficacious of these good works was the mass. More will be said in Chapter 4 about the nature of urban religion. The point to emphasise here is the increase in demand for spiritual services in the later middle ages. In some respects the clergy can be seen as insurance salesmen, offering the security of salvation. Rich individuals could buy masses for themselves; for those who were concerned with, or who could only afford mutuality, membership of a fraternity offered a share in the services of a priest to say masses for the dead. The vast increase in the sale of indulgences, that is, the purchase of promises of exemption from some of the pains of purgatory, is evident from the early thirteenth century onwards; the system offered the prospect of payment by instalment against an uncertain future. The trade in spiritual futures went hand in hand with that in material necessities, for the job of chapman and questor (seller of indulgences) was being combined by the fifteenth century.[88]

By the later middle ages it has been calculated that some 4–6 per cent of the male population of Norwich were priests or members of religious orders. In other regional centres such as York or Lincoln, clergy were equally thick on the ground and numbers were even higher in the university towns of Oxford and Cambridge.[89] There were proportionately far more clergy in large towns than there were in small towns, not only because of the number and size of religious institutions larger towns might house but also because of the unbeneficed secular clergy resident there. The secular clergy were priests who were not in religious orders; the unbeneficed were those who were neither rectors nor vicars of parishes, that is, they had no regular income. Unbeneficed clergy depended on being hired for specific services by fraternities or by individuals and hence inevitably they gravitated to places where lay wealth was concentrated, attaching themselves to specific parishes where possible. By the late fourteenth century the average London parish supported six clergy, the majority of them unbeneficed.[90] It would seem that this large number of chaplains were able to put together enough of an income from performing religious services to keep their heads above water, although it also seems probable that like John Edwyn, chaplain and bow-stringmaker, some supplemented their spiritual earnings with those from more mundane tasks.

For most of the clergy their literacy offered them extra job oppor-tunities in the writing and keeping of documents, so for example they were commonly called on to write and act as executors of wills. In Scot-land it was customary for the secular clergy to act as notaries public, with recognised status as legal keepers of the record and advisers on the law. A man did not have to be in full orders to be able to take on clerical tasks; many who called themselves clerk had only proceeded to minor orders, that is, they were not yet priests who could perform the mass. Like the Wife of Bath's toy-boy jolly Jankyn, they may have taken minor orders as a means of increasing their career prospects, a medieval equivalent of a diploma in management. It was an attractive option for those who wanted to escape from the limited career prospects of manual labour, however skilled. The poet Hoccleve, fed up that he had to 'stowpe and stare upon the schepys skyn' in glum silence, envied the artisans who

talken and singe and make game and play
and forth hyr labour passyth whith gladness[91]

Apart from the fact that he might have felt differently if up to his armpits in tanning liquid, his sentiments do not seem to have been shared by the significant proportion of artisans who actively sought a clerical career for their children.

Although literacy was controlled by the Church, from the thirteenth century onwards an increasing number of administrators were laymen, amongst whom in England and Wales were large numbers of lawyers. As will be discussed later, the legal profession did not become established in Scotland until right at the end of our period. But for England and Wales, Harding emphasises the importance of towns 'in their concentra-tion and nurturing of the professional skills of law and administration'.[92] As administration and the law became more complex, ecclesiastical and secular institutions within towns needed a bank of officials to assist and to represent them. Cathedral cities and county towns were the loci of diocesan and crown courts, bringing in not only a regular flow of lit-igants, but giving encouragement to the provision of permanent legal services in provincial towns. Such services could in fact be the making of a small town. Carmarthen and Caernarfon both prospered in the later middle ages as a result of the large number of permanent officials they supported; Caernarfon was known as a 'town of lawyers'. Here officials used their position to embark on other lucrative options, running taverns, for example; one was even accused of keeping 'a bawdry in the schecker'.[93] The continued and indeed growing importance of county towns as administrative centres could to some extent mitigate the painful effect of the migration of industry to new venues.

Towns were also centres of financial services, albeit of a fairly primitive kind. There were no indigenous bankers as such, but the richest townsmen were both moneylenders and moneychangers. The particular group of townsmen in a position to offer this facility changed over time. In Anglo-Saxon England the right to mint coins was devolved to moneyers who operated in over eighty boroughs. In the chief mints such as London, York, Lincoln or Winchester the profits of the moneyer were sufficiently large to place them in the top echelons of urban society, their position reinforced by their capacity to make loans to the influential. As the Crown assumed greater control over minting and the number of mints was drastically reduced, the influence of the moneyers dwindled. By the thirteenth century the most important moneylenders were the Jews. Their 'phenomenal capital accumulation' was initially fostered by crown interest, and ultimately destroyed by that same interest, for the Crown helped the Jewish community in order to be able to tax it more fiercely.[94] By the 1260s the Jews were ruined; with their usefulness gone, they were dispensable, and were expelled from all those territories controlled by the English Crown in 1290.

Borrowers had therefore to look to other sources for loans. Much has been said already about how the Crown's demands in England led to the emergence of an indigenous group of financiers, made rich on trade. These were men whose power lay not only in their personal fortunes, but also their networking abilities; the rise of William de la Pole was based on his 'ability to borrow huge sums of money' from people who refused to make direct loans to the government.[95] A similar dependence on denizens rather than aliens is evident in late medieval Scotland; a man like Adam Forrester acted as financial agent for nobility and clergy as well as the Crown in the fourteenth century.[96] Reliance on Edinburgh merchants like Forrester for their financial help was yet another factor in reinforcing that town's dominance in the Scottish urban network.

## Conclusion

There were strong similarities between the economies of towns in all parts of the British Isles in the twelfth and thirteenth centuries. One striking unifying factor is the smallness of the majority of British towns in comparison to those on the Continent. This has generally been seen as a peculiarity of British urbanisation, but it may not in fact prove to be quite so distinctive a characteristic as has been assumed. Hilton's comparison of English and French feudal towns draws attention to the similarities rather than the differences between small towns in England and France. It may be that the relatively small number of seriously large towns in the British Isles has tended to persuade historians that a qualitatively different kind of urbanisation was experienced in Britain. But given the close connection that historians are establishing between rural and urban economies, it seems unlikely that the British experience would be unique. Small towns were the essential first points of exchange in a hierarchy of towns which interacted with each other. The place of the town in the hierarchy depended on the level of goods and services it could offer and the distance to which people were prepared to travel in order to obtain these goods and services. Hence the emphasis is primarily on the town as a centre of exchange rather than as a place of manufacture.

Throughout the period there were severe limitations on the growth of the market. Neither in agricultural or craft production was there any radical breakthrough that revolutionised supply, though the cumulative effect of small advances raised output over the long term. Demand, too, was subject to a number of constraints. Up until the mid-fourteenth century a major limitation was the poverty of those who were potential buyers in the mass market. A growing population with an increasing proportion unable to support themselves on the land alone fed the need for the production of basic goods, but it was necessarily an inelastic demand. Long-distance trade existed to fund and supply the goods and services needed by the elite. These generalisations apply to all parts of the British Isles, though the extent to which a network of towns to meet these demands had been established by 1300 varied from region to region. It was most dense in southern England, sparser in Wales, Ireland and southern Scotland, non-existent in the highlands of Scotland.

From the fourteenth century onwards the economies of towns in the different parts of the British Isles show more divergence. Irish towns were the most radically different, as the economy of large parts of the country reverted to Gaelic practice. Trade was concentrated on the export of livestock, hides and fish. Hence despite the greater complexity of urban culture by the fifteenth and early sixteenth centuries, in respect of their economies and the dependence on overseas trade in agricultural produce to fund the spending of the rich, Irish towns recalled English towns of the twelfth century rather than their counterparts around 1500.

Urban economies in late medieval Scotland are open to two very different interpretations. A pessimistic view derives from the figures of overseas trade, which certainly make dismal reading. Most towns, except Edinburgh, lost the most significant part of their overseas trade, forcing their inhabitants to diversify, so that individual urban economies went in different directions. The prevailing view until recently was that this was an uphill and not very successful struggle. However, Gemmill and Mayhew are inclined to be more optimistic about the late medieval Scottish economy. Their study of price levels leads them to conclude that there were 'fairly healthy levels of demand' for most products.[97] Even if there was not a great deal that anyone wanted to take out of Scotland, there were sufficient keen consumers to sustain demand within Scotland. Possibly there was a hidden increase in domestic manufacturing supplying this demand. This more upbeat interpretation does square with the efflorescence of town foundation from the mid-fifteenth century onwards.

But it is a mistake to generalise about the whole period 1350–1500, as is made evident by the more abundant evidence for English towns, where both extremes of economic success and distress can be found. All of the evidence points to there having been an improved standard of living for the majority, but this does not mean that growing spending power in the domestic market was sufficient to compensate for the losses resulting from population decline and economic recession in the fifteenth century. Britnell's study of Colchester led him to conclude that, in that town at least, it was not; Colchester's growth in the later middle ages was not a result of a better and more broadly-based demand in the home market, but rather generated by the growing export trade in cloth.[98] There are problems reconciling this interpretation of the urban economy with the role of a town as a central place, a role which lays emphasis on the level of demand for goods and services in the region served by the town. In contrast, Kowaleski has argued that in Exeter the late medieval boom was achieved in concert with a growth in the economy of its hinterland. The contradictions cannot at present be reconciled.

However, despite the difficulties attached to applying central place theory, it would seem worth pursuing as a useful model of the way that towns interacted with each other and with their regions. More work now needs to be done on how the innovations in the cloth industry affected relationships between towns. Miller and Hatcher distinguish the growth of textile manufacturing in rural areas as 'probably the most original manifestation of economic advance during the central middle ages'.[99] Despite the subsequent importance of industrialised villages in the manufacture of cloth, this manifestation of economic advance did not fatally undermine the role of towns in general, though it did contribute to the rearrangement of the hierarchy in a dramatic way. Towns still served as centres for distribution of the new product and for supplying essentials to the rural artisan. The chapmen could not carry everything. The urban network was just as firmly established in 1500 as it had been in 1300. Whereas large numbers of chartered rural markets had disappeared as the population contracted after the Black Death, towns retained their function as places that offered specialised goods and services. Towns also continued to offer service industries that could not be purveyed by the pedlar and these, particularly those delegated by central government, reinforced the role of county towns, even when other sectors of the economy might be struggling. But in every aspect of its economy, the English provincial town came to be increasingly dependent on, or led by, London. Above all in trade, it was Londoners who had the best access to capital and credit, and whose commercial connections dominated the English urban hierarchy. This concentration of power and resources in London is a theme that will be taken up again in the next chapter, in the context of urban government.

# 3

# URBAN GOVERNMENT

Great pains have been taken so far to impress on the reader that the town should be defined economically in the first instance, rather than as a legal entity. Some backtracking is now called for because legally defined privileges, even if only the most basic right to hold land by the more liberal terms of burgage tenure, were seen by contemporaries as a distinctive element of urban life. The emphasis now placed on the importance of the market as the basis of the urban network came about as a reaction by historians to the stress laid on the legal and constitutional definition of boroughs found in the pioneering works on towns such as Tait's *Medieval English Borough* and Ballard's *British Borough Charters*.[1] It has been demonstrated that to define towns in purely legal terms is not enough. However, the significance now being given to the role of lords in attempting to structure and control the urban network is a reminder that towns were seen by contemporaries as legally distinct entities. This was true of Anglo-Saxon towns as well as those planted in Britain post conquest and colonisation. There was a sense that the business of townspeople was conducted on different terms to those of the surrounding countryside. What were those terms? How distinctive was the urban community legally and administratively; in what respect were towns innovative, and in what ways did they act as a brake on social change?

The extent of the privileges granted to townspeople might be pretty minimal, nor can any necessary correlation be made between the size of the town and the extent of such privilege; no clear equation can be made between institutional sophistication and a town's place in the urban hierarchy. But it is helpful not to expect too much order and consistency. Certainly towns did self-consciously copy one another's constitutions. The best known of these packages of rights were the privileges of the

Norman town of Breteuil applied as the basis for the reorganisation of a number of English and Welsh seigneurial towns. Customs duplicating those of Newcastle make up an important element of the Scottish Burgh Laws (*Leges Burgorum*), a consolidation of regulations relating to Scottish towns which was compiled over the twelfth and thirteenth centuries and which, in theory, constituted a model for all burghs. There was, by the thirteenth century, also a Court of the Four Burghs in Scotland, convened by the leading towns, and which claimed appeal rights in urban law. But in reality towns ended up with distinctive administrations: to take just one instance, the privileges of both Ruthin and Caernarfon were derived from those of Hereford; in Ruthin, unusually, the Welsh were equal with the English, but Caernarfon was characterised by extreme distrust of, and discrimination against, the Welsh.[2]

The apparently bewildering variety of urban liberties makes more sense if it is understood in the light of who had access to these liberties and who controlled them. Who was running the towns is just as much an issue as how they were run. Medieval urban institutions served both to protect the profit of the lord and to enhance the livings of those who lived in the town. These objectives might be rendered more complex: the interests of the immediate lord and the Crown might diverge; equally there might be several interest groups among the townspeople pulling in different directions. Existing institutions, offices and associations were adapted in response to the tensions between these different interest groups. Whether such changes were achieved peaceably or in the teeth of opposition, and how far they went, depended on local circumstances. But in order to keep explanations as clear as possible, this chapter will first need to consider who the burgesses were, and the institutions through which government was exercised, before going on to examine the circumstances in which those institutions evolved over time and the personnel of government.

## Burgesses

The privileges granted to townspeople were intended to make them better able to trade: freedom of movement, that is personal freedom, a right to be impleaded in the town's courts, a degree of control over their own property, and an economic advantage over outsiders constituted the core of these privileges. Details of what these economic privileges meant were given in the previous chapter. But just who was going to benefit from these advantages? Early charters show the process of working out just who qualified as burgesses and what was involved in burgess status. The personal freedom of townspeople contrasted with the servile bonds that bound a peasant who was unfree to his or her lord. Indeed this contrast was specifically referred to in those town charters that allowed personal freedom to any serf that had remained a year and a day within the town without being apprehended. However, the possession of such personal freedom was initially conceived as a form of tenure, burgage tenure open to men and women, whether granted informally or by charter. The urban tenement was held from the lord at a fixed rent, often standardised in twelfth-century England at 12*d*. The tenement was then under the control of the tenant who might bequeath, give or sell the property freely.

There were some caveats: Scottish burgage tenure was somewhat more restrictive in some cases, where alienation of the tenement had to be to heirs; on the other hand kirset allowed the tenant to hold a property rent free for three years in Scotland, in order to get established. Widows were also protected during their lifetimes by being given rights in a proportion of the estate whilst they remained single. Not all lords were prepared in the first instance to concede the principle of free burgage in its entirety. Before the thirteenth century some services might attach to the tenement, in particular defensive obligations, as was the case with some of the newly planted Welsh castle boroughs. Such additional obligations were increasingly infrequent and had disappeared in theory by the thirteenth century, though some lords found it exceptionally difficult to tear themselves away from the idea. Lists of leases drawn up by the Abbot of Evesham in the late fourteenth century, which take in both rural and urban tenements and their associated obligations, show that even at this late date the Abbot was attempting to keep control of the land market in the small town around his abbey. Other lords can still be found imposing servile dues on burgesses well into the fourteenth century, as was the case for the villein burgesses of Shipston on Stour.[3]

The neat equation between the privileged inhabitants of a town and those holding by burgess tenure was not the most appropriate way of identifying and defining a commercial community. The way in which the idea of personal freedom as inherent in urban residence became detached from burgess tenure was probably pragmatic. From the outset there were always likely to be migrants who could not afford a full lease. They can be seen arriving in the small town of Halesowen in the thirteenth and early fourteenth centuries, where the burgesses turned their tenements into lodging houses, acting as guarantors of good behaviour of new arrivals.[4] Attempts by the town to evict the unsatisfactory proved useless; they simply reappeared. Most men and women coming to a small town were from nearby villages and their status must have been well known. The assumption must be that in a time of rising population no lord was likely to pursue serfs considered superfluous to requirements; perhaps this may go some way towards accounting for the fact that a majority of small-town immigrants were women. Only in the post-Black Death period was there apparently any strenuous effort made to retrieve rural labour from towns. Well before this the idea that 'town air made free' on its own accord without the assistance of a particular form of tenure had become established, though there were still, of course, exceptions: the Irish in Dublin, living under Irish law, generally had villein status in the thirteenth century.

If all townspeople were free, were all going to benefit equally from the economic privileges offered to attract migrants? Initially such privileges inhered in the possession of burgage tenure, but as with personal freedom, the association of economic advantage with a particular form of tenure became detached, although echos of the principle remained in the Scottish burgh. In Scotland the importance of having a physical stake in the town was underlined by the rule that relatives could prevent a burgess from selling inherited land, except in the most desperate circumstances. The urban land market was freer in England. There the very freedom with which plots could be transferred would inevitably undermine the suitability of burgage tenure as a basis for inclusion within the urban community. Tenements were accumulated by both laity and clergy for a variety of reasons and the size and significance of the urban rentier class varied over time, but there was always a tendency towards the investment in real property as a form of security. Whereas the ground rent to the lord remained fixed and increasingly nominal, sub-leasing of whole or divided tenements could be done at an economic rent, reflecting the market value of the property and giving, it was hoped, a regular if not spectacular return on investment. The situation was recognised in a charter to Cardiff of the late twelfth century: 'if a burgess has two burgages and wishes to let one of them to another, the lessor can, if he wish, grant the same liberty to the hirer of the said burgage, as he himself has, and the hirer shall enjoy such liberty'.[5] By the later middle ages the urban merchant or artisan was as likely to be the sub-tenant of an ecclesiastical institution as the holder of a burgage. But by that time the equation of burgess tenure and the right to trade free of toll had long since parted company.

One explicit way of delineating the privileged trading community in the twelfth century was through the establishment of a guild merchant. These were the exception rather than the rule in English towns, but in the newly planted towns of Scotland the guild merchant seems to have been included automatically in the foundation charters, though whether all these guilds materialised in reality is another matter. Who could be a member of this guild? It was obviously a matter of pressing importance, for the earliest urban administrative records we possess, dating from the late twelfth century, are lists of guild members from Leicester and Dublin.[6] Membership was not always restricted to townspeople: the twelfth-century burgesses of Pembroke extended the right to 'all merchants of the county of Pembroke'.[7] Nor was the guild merchant initially wholly socially exclusive, but drew its membership from among small-scale artisans as well as the larger wholesalers: carpenters as well as vintners in Shrewsbury. On the other hand the guild in Andover was a two-tiered affair, with those in the higher tier being very much more equal than those in the lower.[8]

But the guild merchant did not prove to be the commonest or most enduring way of defining the trading community. No town was going to allow trading privileges to all comers, but they varied considerably in the criteria they set as to which inhabitants should benefit. Colchester is an example of a particularly generous town where burgess status and the right to trade freely could be claimed by any man born in the borough. Other towns were a great deal more restrictive. The commonest form of restriction was by limiting access to the title of burgess, so that the free burgesses with privileged access to trade came to be a minority. This move can be seen to be happening in Scotland by the late twelfth and early thirteenth centuries. Equally, in England it was during the thirteenth century that a more explicit and restricted definition of urban freedom emerged: it could be acquired through purchase or by inheriting the right to participate in the town's economic and political life. Sons and, far less frequently, daughters of freemen could inherit the freedom without charge; those gaining access by apprenticeship paid a small fee; anyone else could buy themselves in at varying cost.

Quite why the franchise became so restricted is, as Dobson says, a 'mysterious problem'.[9] It could be associated with the growing complexity of town government and the increasing physical size of towns. Not only did the freedom give commercial advantage, it defined those who made up the effective political community in the town. Hence the restriction of the franchise could be seen as a reasonable response to the feeling that those who were shouldering the costs of urban rule should benefit in some particular way. The political element of the franchise seems to be underlined by the fact that licences to trade on an annual basis continued to be given to those not free of the town. Just how reasonable in contemporary terms this arrangement actually was depends on how wide the access to the privilege of the franchise was; often it was very restricted, and it looks as though the restricted franchise evolved to protect the interests of the more substantial townspeople, be they merchants or the more successful artisans. The widening of the franchise in many towns in the later middle ages does not imply any sea change in outlook towards a more generous policy of inclusion. As will be seen, the extension of its scope came at a time when urban government was becoming more highly structured and oligarchical, so that the flood of new freemen were not going to gain any significant political privilege. Rather, the franchise came to be used as a source of revenue, for of course the newcomers had to buy their way in. Continued manipulation of the franchise to give a desirable fiscal and social outcome seems evident in the Dublin freemen's rolls of the late fifteenth century. Under economic pressure Dublin, like other Irish towns, needed to recruit the sort of substantial men who were potential office holders. A total prohibition was put on any Irish who had not lived in the city for 12 years; few artisans were made free by apprenticeship and a big proportion of this category were merchants. In contrast, large numbers of husbandmen and yeomen living outside the city were allowed to purchase the freedom.[10]

How far the town extended geographically also posed a dilemma. Who had jurisdiction over the inhabitants of suburbs and what their status was in respect of urban privilege, were pressing points in those twelfth- and thirteenth-century towns which were growing physically very rapidly indeed, and in a culture where justice was an important source of revenue. It might depend on what privileges were being claimed. In late thirteenth-century Bury the burgesses were incensed by the fact that a man could be hanged for robbery because he lived outside the town gate, whereas if he lived inside he would have been tried under a different law and escaped with his life. However, as the Abbey chronicler Joscelin smugly pointed out, 'the burgesses still maintain that suburban dwellers ought not to be free from toll in the market unless they are members of the guild merchant'.[11] Borough boundaries might be formally redefined, as in the case of Brecon, where a late thirteenth-century charter incorporated the new substantial suburbs into the twelfth-century town. A far more protracted and expensive negotiation was involved in the extension of the jurisdiction of Bristol and its suburbs, for the town was up against more deeply entrenched rival jurisdictions.[12] New walls might be built to signify inclusion, but even in colonising settlements a wall did not constitute the legal boundary of the town. Dublin is a particularly notable example of a town with a small walled area, with the majority of the population in the thirteenth century living in the suburbs.

Nor was the town necessarily under the control of one lord or one jurisdiction. Older-established towns might be divided between competing jurisdictions. The most extreme example was Durham, which was in fact not one town but five separate ones, independent communities with their own sense of identity.[13] Racial discrimination in Ireland meant that, for example, in Kilkenny, there was a separate Irish borough with its own courts and officials. Competing jurisdictions within the town more usually took the form of liberties, enclaves of private jurisdiction, with varying degrees of privilege, where the town's authority and judicial powers could not run. London at the time of the Norman Conquest was riddled with independent jurisdictions that were only gradually eliminated by the combined pressure of civic aspiration and royal interference. The Crown itself kept jurisdiction in key urban areas such as the environs of the castle in a strategic site, but the most significant liberties belonged to the Church. Properties around major ecclesiastical institutions could form an enclave where the inhabitants could behave with relative impunity as far as urban by-laws were concerned. A particularly notorious example was the liberty by Westminster Abbey, which harboured debtors and miscreants, people with good reason to be reluctant to step outside the protection of the sanctuary.[14] The legal significance of franchises had dwindled by the later middle ages as the Crown increasingly elaborated the scope of royal justice, but some remained as a thorn in the flesh of self-conscious civic authorities.

## Institutions of Urban Government

The matter of conflicting jurisdictions leads on to the whole question of how towns were run. Clearly urban government was not static but changed considerably between the twelfth and sixteenth centuries. It also developed in different directions in different parts of the British

Isles. So this section will deal first with the institutions of urban government as conceived and put in place in the twelfth century. It will then go on to outline the changes that took place between the thirteenth and early sixteenth centuries. Whether these changes were achieved peacefully or in the teeth of opposition will then be discussed in the next section on governors and governed.

Twelfth-century urban government has to be understood in the context of lordship, whether that lord be the king, or a lay or ecclesiastical magnate. Lordship entailed rights over people as well as land, that is, it included the right to oversee justice and the keeping of the peace, as well as the rights associated with the ownership of land. In this context urban government was seen essentially as a system of law enforcement and the key institutions were the courts. Within the courts, public and private jurisdiction, criminal and civil, were not initially at all clearly distinguished. Very broadly speaking civil jurisdiction, such as debt cases or those relating to land transfer, derived from a lord's territorial right. Public order jurisdiction over minor offences, such as wounding, or the breaches of national legislation (assizes) on the price of bread and ale, was delegated from the Crown, and in these cases the presiding officer of the court acted as the Crown's representative (though he was a representative whose right to the office was, in the twelfth century, often hereditary, seen as an integral part of lordship). There was a limit to the extent to which a lord might exercise rights over public jurisdiction. Some peacekeeping functions were reserved entirely to the Crown, those 'touching the king' – treason obviously, but also serious crimes, known as felonies, which disturbed the king's peace: murder, arson, thefts of large sums, robbery. These could only be tried before one of the Crown's justices.

But most cases were presented in the first instance in the same urban court, a court which was not fundamentally different in structure to those operating in rural areas. And although there were a myriad of local variations, in neither England or Scotland was there a significant difference in the nature of the law practised in town and country. In Scotland the introduction of burghs paralleled the feudal settlement of the countryside, both based in the same law. In Wales and Ireland the towns were more obviously intended to spearhead the introduction of a new law, and Welsh and Gaelic law continued to operate in rural areas; Welsh law was ultimately overwhelmed by the end of the period, Gaelic law, conversely, came to invade the increasingly isolated towns of south and west Ireland.

For some twelfth-century English towns the urban court might indeed be no more than a manorial court. Where a small town emerged from an active trading community, before it was formally constituted as a borough, the existing institutions of rural lordship were simply adapted to new circumstances. In a few cases, despite subsequent and sometimes spectacular growth, a town might never legally become a borough and might continue to be run through the manor court right through to the sixteenth century. This was the case with Westminster, where the simplicity of the institutions of government belied a sophisticated administration under the control of the town's wealthiest inhabitants. Rather more complex was the administration of Southwark, which coalesced out of a series of manors as a major suburb of London south of the river, but which continued to be run by five separate manorial courts into the sixteenth century.[15]

The borough or burgh court was the equivalent to the manor court in the newly founded, or newly chartered, towns; it was often referred to as the 'portmanmoot' in England, the word 'port' being a synonym for borough. The court was presided over by an official initially called the reeve, but subsequently and more commonly known as the bailiff in England or bailie in Scotland, who was appointed by and answerable to the lord, either king (via the sheriff) or magnate. The principle that the inhabitants of the borough or burgh should only be brought before the urban court was an important one, as it meant that urban custom, both on tenurial matters and on commercial transactions, which together made up the bulk of the court's business, would determine judgements. Hence in a newly founded borough the court's jurisdiction was explicitly distinguished from the manor out of which it was carved.

In England the borough court was able to handle cases relating to public order by virtue of the fact that it also functioned as a hundred court. The hundred was the basic unit of local government to which policing powers were attached and which dealt out summary justice for minor misdemeanours. In rural areas it would normally cover several settlements, but for convenience sake boroughs were generally deemed to be hundreds in their own right. The men of the hundred were mutually responsible for peacekeeping and were answerable for their effectiveness in doing so at extended sessions of the hundred court held twice or three times a year. Just who they were answerable to depended on whether the jurisdiction of the hundred was in the hands of the Crown or had been granted away by the king to a lord. If the town were held direct from the Crown these big lawhundred sessions were presided over by the sheriff on his 'tourn', that is, his regular tour of all the hundreds in his jurisdiction. If the hundred jurisdiction were in the hands of the lord the extended session, called the court leet, was presided over by the lord's steward.

At these sessions the townsmen had to answer satisfactorily a list of questions posed by the sheriff or steward, including an inquiry into any felonies committed. The indicted felons, if they could be apprehended, were then sent to gaol until one of the king's justices arrived in the locality to deal with them: the trial by the king's justices was known, logically, as gaol delivery. The lawhundred or court leet was also the opportunity to check or 'view' the effectiveness of the system of frankpledge, an arrangement whereby the townsmen were grouped in tens or twelves, responsible for each other's behaviour. Whereas in most boroughs the hundred jurisdiction was more or less coextensive with the borough, the Anglo-Saxon legacy in a few larger towns was more complex. Most notably, London was divided into several hundreds, some of them (called sokes) in private hands. By the eleventh century the city had already become administratively the equivalent of a shire, with the borough reeve doubling as the sheriff of Middlesex.

In Scotland the burgh court was probably as old as the burgh itself, but this has to be an assumption because there are no records of burgh courts before the thirteenth century. When the urban court does emerge into the records it has similar outlines to those of English provincial towns. It was held by the *prepositi* or bailies of the town. In royal towns the immediate supervision of these officials was probably initially the responsibility of the sheriff, but this was not always the case. Sheriffdoms were established in a piecemeal fashion, so that important towns like Aberdeen were founded in places beyond the jurisdiction of a sheriff. But the supervisory role of the sheriff seems already to have been superseded by the late twelfth century; it is likely that the royal chamberlain was by then the crown officer responsible for the burghs.[16] The oversight of Scottish burghs of regality by the eyres (annual circuits) of the chamberlain is in fact an explicit expression of the Crown's financial motives in founding towns in the first place. Like English borough courts, the Scottish burgh courts were given authority over petty crimes and civil disputes. Three times a year a larger congregation called the head court was assembled; this was the occasion for those committing serious crimes to be indicted. Jurisdiction over more serious crimes lay with royal justiciars, appointed from among the barons, who travelled the regions on circuits to sit in judgement on those indicted at head courts.

Because the court was the normal arena for discussion, it was used as a vehicle for arbitration and administration as much as for the resolution of cases in favour of one party or another; indeed actions were started in order to define the accepted parameters of behaviour or to get the parties moving as much as in the expectation of a definitive settlement. But, however largely borough or burgh courts featured, urban government was not wholly encompassed by their dealings. Early urban charters detail another form of association, the guild merchant, already encountered as a means for counting in those with commercial clout. The word 'guild' embraces a variety of associations and was used very flexibly; hence guilds make various appearances in this book in different guises. Here they are considered as vehicles of local administration.

The guild could operate as a talking shop where the common ground for membership was business, and which could act as a forum for commercial information and decision making, supplementing the administration of the burgh court. It is probable that the charters that certify to their emergence from the twelfth century onwards were more affirmations of associations that were already functioning than instruments for the creation of new institutions. The guild merchant might also have its own court to control the activities of its members in commercial matters. The guild court could operate in parallel with the borough court, as is particularly well documented for Leicester, though the boundary between the jurisdictions was not clear-cut.[17] The distinction was further blurred in the frequent cases where the chief members of the guild were interchangeable with the officers of the borough administration. The link between the two bodies was made explicit in early Scottish charters when the chief officer of the burgh was also to be the chief officer of the guild merchant, though just how significant the guild merchant was in twelfth- and thirteenth-century Scottish towns remains disputed; it probably varied from place to place, depending on the way those in power chose to use the institutional structures available to them.

The thirteenth to the fifteenth centuries saw some radical changes in the sort of business dealt with by urban administrations and in the way that business was carried out, and it is to these we must now turn. In considering these changes it is helpful to isolate three factors: the growth of the economy and the commercialisation of society; the move by towns to acquire more autonomy; and the centralisation of government. Not all these factors applied with equal force everywhere, and the experience of those parts of the British Isles effectively controlled by the English differs in some measure to that of the Scots. However, the first factor, the growth of the economy and the commercialisation of exchange, did apply throughout the British Isles, and meant the proliferation and specialisation of urban courts in order to deal with the growing amount of business. This meant at the minimum more regular meetings of the burgh or borough court: by the early fourteenth century in Colchester the hundred court was already sitting every fortnight; in Aberdeen the burgh court was meeting every few days by the end of the fourteenth century.[18]

It was not only the amount of business that multiplied the tasks of the bailiffs and their assistants, but also the extent to which they were expected and required to interfere in that business as towns became more and more preoccupied with, and charged with, the regulation of diverse aspects of urban life. The principle behind much of this regulation was one of consumer protection, and of the limitation of excess profit, and much of it was directed at the food market. Here, as well as enforcing their own by-laws, bailiffs were responsible for the overseeing of the national assizes which, both in English and Scottish law, laid down the quality and price of dietary staples, bread and ale, or regulated weights and measures. Infringement of these national assizes was theoretically meant to be handled at the triennial leet court, law hundred or head court. This might prove unsatisfactory in a town of any size, and individual towns developed their own solutions for nailing offenders as quickly as possible: by noting down names at the regular borough courts, or by convening ad hoc inquests to pursue particularly outrageous instances of abuse.

The growth of business usually also meant the development of specialised courts for dealing with specific types of business. Merchant courts handled the business of people in a hurry; so, for example, in Scotland decisions in these courts had to be made by the third tide. Similarly, rapid decisions had to be made in the courts specific to fairs and they, like the merchant courts, might be known as pie-powder sessions, in reference to the dusty-footed merchants, packed and ready to go, who gained by their quick procedures. Land transactions might also be hived off into specialised sessions, with registries of deeds established to cope with the demands of what, by the thirteenth century, had become in some towns a sophisticated property market.

The second impetus to change was also a response to the growing size and prosperity of towns. This was the move by certain towns to acquire more autonomy from their lords, control over the election of the personnel of urban government and urban finances and pressure to extend their authority over the liberties that existed within their bounds. A significant step forward in the acquisition of administrative independence was to grant the townspeople the right to elect their own bailiffs, a process that was often accompanied by the granting to the town of more control over its financial affairs. The town bought from the lord the right to pay a fixed sum annually, known as the fee farm, or (in Scotland) the feu farm, in lieu of all other payments: rents, market dues, fines and taxes; in return the town assumed control over internal financial administration.

The first recorded fee farms in England were those paid by London and Lincoln in 1130. The burgesses of Richmond shortly after arranged to pay £29 a year to Count Alan of Brittany in lieu of all dues.[19] However, it was not until the late twelfth or thirteenth centuries that grants of the fee farm became anything but the exception, and even then Alan of Brittany did not provide a precedent for other seigneurial lords; most fee farms were granted to royal towns. Similar grants were being made to royal towns in Ireland over the same period, with Dublin holding from the Crown for an annual fee of 200 marks from 1215.[20] It was probably during the thirteenth century that Scottish towns also began to farm their revenues, initially leasing the right to do so annually, but with feu farms being bought outright and in perpetuity during the fourteenth century, and in particular from 1357 onwards, when the Crown was desperate for cash, as a result of the ransom demand for David II, held in English captivity.

The delegation of financial responsibility was accompanied by the emergence of a new official to head the urban administration. In Scotland this official was called the alderman or provost; in England and Wales the equivalent post was that of the mayor. Just how radical the mayoralty was originally conceived to be will be considered later. But here it can be noted that, although not generally formally recognised in England till the late thirteenth century, mayors were tacitly accepted well before that, both in royal and seigneurial towns. This does suggest that they were assimilated fairly readily into the urban hierarchy because they had proved to be useful. Indeed, the mayor might be expected to act overtly as crown agent. In Welsh towns belonging to the Crown, where the constable of the castle had acted as bailiff, the roles of constable and mayor in turn came to be amalgamated.

The status of the mayor varied from place to place. In a seigneurial town, where control was vested firmly in the lord's steward or bailiff, the post might have little more than ceremonial significance. The fact that in the later middle ages the chief court of Aberdeen was still held by the bailies rather than the mayor suggests that elsewhere the power of the mayor might also still be strongly circumscribed by the burgh traditions. However, particularly in larger towns, the mayor did become a figure of considerable power. He assumed the role of chief executive of the town, and acted as the most senior officer in the borough courts.

The mayor was an elected official and, given the amount of power he might wield, a crucial issue was obviously who elected him, though as with the election of the bailiffs, there is often no certain evidence on this point before the later middle ages. It was most probably a restricted electorate: only the 'gud men of the toune, the whilk aw to be lele and of gud fame' were to be entrusted with this task.[21] The 'gud men' were a self-selected group, whose composition came to be more explicitly defined by the later middle ages, so that by the late thirteenth century the election of the mayor in Berwick was in the hand of 24 'worthy men'.[22] This arrangement was made in order to avoid controversy, that is, the unwanted interference of the lesser sort. It seems likely that these 24 were the same worthy men as made up the council of the burgh.

For at the same time that urban communities were developing the office of mayor, they also began experimenting with more formal bodies for consultation and supervision of administration. Those bodies were usually one or more circles of advisers, multiples of 12, the earliest evidence of which comes from Ipswich dating from 1200, where in the self-conscious flush of novelty the town clerk wrote a detailed account of how the council was constituted and appointed. There the whole town (that is, the political community) elected two bailiffs and four coroners, and then went on to choose 12 portmen as a governing council. The portmen were clearly not intended as a popular counterbalance to the key officials, for the two bailiffs were also coroners and all four coroners were portmen.[23] Ipswich was unusual in documenting a process which normally evolved by stages, unrecorded, and where charters of institution were merely ratifications of existing arrangements. So although a council had appeared in the records for Dublin by 1229, and in other large towns by the late thirteenth century, they were probably effectively operative from rather earlier. Similarly, the late appearance of councils in small towns can be taken as formalising the power of those who had customarily run the town, hence the apparently late emergence of councils in Welsh towns: in 1421 12 aldermen were created to assist the mayor of Cardiff, and the town council of Brecon emerged into the records in the early sixteenth century.[24]

Berwick was the model for many Scottish towns and, as we have seen, had instituted a council by the late thirteenth century, but the persistent vitality of the guild merchant in Scotland suggests that in reality this latter was often the more potent decision-making assembly. Certainly it was a well-entrenched body in Aberdeen, where surviving records from the late fourteenth century onwards show the guild court ruling on matters of trade and commerce.[25] In Dunfermline in the fifteenth century the guild was putting in urban infrastructure, building roads and upgrading the port, dispensing more money that the burgh court.[26] The decisive shift in authority from guild to council in Scotland seems to have come during the late fifteenth or even the sixteenth centuries. In contrast, in England, guilds merchant faded out during the thirteenth century, having given way to more elaborate urban constitutions. It seems very likely that it was the agitation by the members of the English guilds merchant for more explicit control of urban government that rendered the guild itself redundant, the key personnel of the guilds coming to be well entrenched in civic office and on the town councils. The merchant guilds which emerge in English towns of the fourteenth and fifteenth centuries had different and far more specifically sectional commercial functions than the earlier guilds merchant.

As well as developing their own structures of government, the desire for autonomy led townspeople to agitate for more independence of action in respect of their lords. For English towns this was symbolised in the gradual exclusion of the sheriff, the Crown's agent, from interference in the town's business. When a town acquired the right of return of writ, this meant that it was the town itself and not the sheriff that had the power to receive, respond to and act on writs of the Crown within the area of its jurisdiction. This looks on the face of it as if towns were thus getting more independent of central control. However, the fact that this right came to be imposed on larger towns by royal initiative suggests that it was a matter of convenience for the Crown rather than being a major concession. What in fact was taking place was a profound change in the relationship between the Crown and local jurisdictions. This brings us to the third factor involved in the development of urban administration, the centralisation of government and the extension of the authority of the royal courts. This third factor had by far the greatest impact in England, so England will have to be dealt with first before turning to other parts of the British Isles.

During the late twelfth and thirteenth centuries there was a vast increase in the jurisdiction of the English Crown, so that by 1300 all major cases in both criminal and civil law were heard in the royal courts, before professional judges. So, for example, in civil litigation, all cases concerning title to freehold land were to be begun by royal writ and taken before the royal justices; the same came to apply to actions relating to movables and debts of over 40s. The effect was to remove great swathes of business from local courts such as the hundred court, from the jurisdiction of the sheriff, and from the private courts in the hands of lords, though larger boroughs might have some of this jurisdiction delegated back to them, where it related specifically to urban tenure or to commercial matters.

The same process of centralisation and delegation can be seen in the criminal law. As the number of cases reserved to the Crown multiplied, a new officer, the coroner, was introduced to assist the sheriff, appearing in boroughs from c.1200 onwards. Coroners were crown officials, but were chosen from among the townsmen and were an important link between the local and the central courts. Their remit in practice was to record felonies, particularly homicide and suicide, and present the record of those felonies to the Crown's justices when they came into the district, with powers of gaol delivery over waiting felons. That wait became longer and longer as the burden of cases before the itinerant justices multiplied and their progress round the country became slower and more cumbersome.

By the early fourteenth century various experiments had already been made to try and improve the situation. Special commissions of gaol delivery were sent out, some of which employed the leaders of the urban community along with the rural gentry. The ultimate solution was to delegate gaol delivery permanently to local worthies, and a new office, keeper of the peace, subsequently justice of the peace, or JP, was developed, probably the single most significant change to the criminal justice system in the later middle ages. By the late fourteenth century the office of JP was permanently vested in the mayor and bailiffs of the larger English towns. As well as the authority that mayor and bailiffs now had to sit in judgement on more serious crimes, the office of justice of the peace also gave them control over the labour legislation which was passed in the latter part of the fourteenth century, legislation aimed at keeping down wages and restricting immigration at a time of labour shortage.

The final layer of authority that a town might obtain was to become a county in its own right, with the mayor and bailiffs taking over all the remaining responsibilities of the sheriff. Bristol was the first provincial town to achieve this in 1373. Not all towns reached these dizzy heights by a long chalk; by the 1460s only eight more had been made into counties.

The full battery of powers as described here tended to be reserved for royal towns. Seigneurial towns generally could not aspire to such independence. Between the smallest seigneurial towns with minimal jurisdictional rights and the most self-consciously pompous cities, there was what can seem a rather daunting variety of practice. This makes generalisation rather hazardous; at any one time permutations of local practice, tenaciously defended liberties and delegated authority gave a different nuance to the powers exercised by town governments. Within England the overall pattern was one of the centralisation of judicial powers and their delegation to local representatives. But crown authority, manifested in an increasingly complex and sophisticated legal system, was dependent on local officials for its implementation. From the perspective of the urban elite, the changes institutionalised the control that they had over town government. They also served to reinforce the horizontal bonds that developed between the urban elite and their rural counterparts, a shared identity based in part on a shared function in the state judicial machinery. It was a solution to the pressure put on the Crown by the scale of government business and the demand from what was, by the fourteenth century, a 'widening political society', to have an active part in that business.[27] Whether this meant more effective peacekeeping is still open to debate. The impartial operation of JPs depended on whether they were adequately controlled from above or whether they could pursue an overtly partisan line with impunity.

Local government and the delivery of justice changed far less in Scotland. The centralised supervision of the finances of towns of regality by the chamberlain continued throughout the middle ages, but there were no moves to extend central government intervention in burghal affairs beyond this. Some burghs were able to extend their powers in criminal jurisdiction from the late fourteenth century onwards, by being given authority equivalent to that of the sheriff. This included the right to deal with thieves caught red-handed, or unpremeditated homicide cases, though the most serious offences were still reserved to justiciars. But there was no centralisation of the judicial process in the way that there was in England; the delivery of justice in Scotland remained local and amateur in that the execution of the most serious cases remained in the hands of itinerant justiciars and of sheriffs drawn from the magnates, and not in the hands of professional lawyers.

Much of Wales remained under marcher lordships until the end of the period, and here too there was little change in the structure of government. Although the lords themselves became increasingly identified with the political establishment at Westminster, and indeed many of the lordships fell into the hands of the Crown, the administrative peculiarity of the marcher lordships was unaltered. Only with the incorporation of Wales into the government of England in 1536 were the administrative and judicial arrangements of the two countries fully brought into line. However, in those parts of Wales directly supervised by the Crown, that is, the area hitherto governed by Welsh princes that was taken into crown hands after the 1282–83 revolt, the towns were made the foci of increasingly intrusive government, with a corresponding elaboration of adminstrative and judicial personnel. Whereas royal control became more extensive in Wales, orchestrated through the towns, the reverse was the case in Ireland. In the thirteenth century the same centralising measures that had been taken in England were applied to Ireland, but the shrinking of colonised territory meant that they operated with diminishing effect.

Irrespective of the part of the British Isles in which a town lay, by the fifteenth century there were a vast number of regulations to be either obeyed or flouted by townspeople. The extensive elaboration of urban authority brought with it the multiplication of urban officials. This was true in Scottish towns as well as the more elaborately governed English towns, for economic growth on its own called in the need for more supervision. In addition to mayor, bailiffs or sheriffs, and coroners, the more complex finances of larger towns required one or more chamberlains. Clerks were needed to record town business and lawyers to maximise revenue. At a lower level there were a formidable number of minor officials, even in small towns without extensive rights of self-government. Constables were put in charge of peacekeeping and controlling nuisances on their patch. There were ale-tasters, bridge wardens, gatekeepers, gaolers; there was even canine assistance – the London Bridge accounts record regular payments for food for the bridge guard-dogs.[28]
At every turn people found town councils increasingly concerned to regulate their behaviour: to commandeer them for local police duties and to eavesdrop on potentially subversive conversations; to chivvy them into repairing the pavement outside their houses and to dispose properly of rubbish; to control dangerous dogs and to keep their other livestock properly penned. Food retailers came under the closest scrutiny, with urban officials gunning for butchers in particular. It was an offence in early sixteenth-century Aberdeen to fail to supply the town with meat, but also an offence to sell the meat before the carcasses had

been checked. In a number of towns it was an offence for butchers to fail to put tallow and hides on the open market; butchers could not act as tanners in case they were fencing stolen cattle. Butchers were to keep their pigs off the street and not to throw offal into public places and watercourses. Personnel were checked too: the Aberdeen butchers' apprentices were not allowed to carry knives unless they were employed in carving meat.[29] Whether all this regulation was effectively enforced must be debatable, given the number of times much of it was reiterated, but it was in place to be used tactically if needed. Implementation would depend in large measure on how many of the town's inhabitants were committed to the values enshrined in these regulations and how many were actively drafted in on the side of enforcing them. It is possible to get the impression that a very substantial proportion of the respectable burgesses of the town, artisans as well as merchants and professionals, were actively bound into the process of urban government, and contributory to the sense of pride and civic worth that was manifested in the multiplication of urban records and the elaboration of urban rituals. It has already been suggested that the primary beneficiaries were the urban elite. What needs to be addressed now, therefore, is whether medieval towns did operate as relatively harmonious wholes. How were these urban liberties achieved, and to whose advantage did they work? Was there such a thing as an urban community?

## Governors and Governed

The involvement of urban government in so many aspects of people's lives does raise the question of who was giving the instructions and who was doing the obeying. So far, what has been outlined is the basic structure of urban government. How did it actually work? Who ran the town; did the composition of the ruling group change, and were they challenged from inside or outside the town? What were the relationships of the town with its lord or the king, and were urban liberties acquired by a process of negotiation or a forced concession? In the history of any one town a variety of factors were likely to come into operation, as different sections of the urban community prospered and as political power at the centre changed its priorities. Hence to try and give a narrative account of why urban liberties were developed would be to end up in a mass of conflicting details. Instead, it is probably more helpful to look at the relationship between interest groups to see the ways in which they might be worked out.

*Towns and their lords*

The terms of urban foundation imply a symbiotic relationship between the burgesses and the lord, designed to advance the profitability of both. There is, of course, plenty of evidence to show that some towns had very tense relationships with their lords at some or occasionally at all times in the period between the twelfth and early sixteenth centuries. However, the tendency current among historians is to emphasise the extent to which arbitration and negotiation were the means by which the relationship was readjusted.

The most powerful lord was the Crown, but in some respects the Crown was also the more distant, in that it was readier to grant the forms of local autonomy than were seigneurial lords. In the twelfth century these grants were given with a certain amount of grudging suspicion and were likely to be rescinded. The increasing number of towns acquiring a measure of independent government in England under Richard I and John was related to the growing need of the king for money, money that the towns, and particularly London, could levy and mobilise.

The communal movement of the late twelfth century erupted in London in response to extreme fiscal demands. There had been some precursors. York, Gloucester and Oxford had tried and failed to form communes in the 1170s. What those seeking to establish a commune aspired to was the creation of a sworn association with an elected head, the mayor, that would stand in independent relationship with the Crown and which was protected from crown interference. Reynolds suggests that the dangers to the Crown were more perceived than actual, the novelty of the legal form rather than its revolutionary potential.[30] Certainly the personnel involved were restricted; those participating in the creation of the London commune of the 1190s were a 'tiny elite'.[31] But although at least one claimed that the city 'shall have no king but their mayor', the reality was a great deal less dramatic. The commune stood in relation to a powerful and centralising monarchy from which it could not assert its independence in the manner of the continental communes from which it took its model; the law that was to run within the town was the Crown's law. Reynolds argues that communes symbolised 'burgess solidarity' rather than revolutionary claims to independence; such solidarity would only be couched in radical terms when exacerbated by crown interference or incompetence. Although ostensibly reluctant to grant recognition to communes, the *de facto* acceptance of a degree of urban autonomy and the tacit acceptance of the mayor provided a compromise that avoided the inflammatory term of a commune. Status could be given to self-conscious urban elites while the office of mayor could be used as the agent of communication with the Crown.

As the previous section has shown, subsequent acquisitions of privilege by towns were often achieved with the co-operation of the Crown and at times by the active implementation of crown policy. Nevertheless, English kings showed themselves very ready to suspend urban privileges where towns appeared to challenge royal authority. This was particularly the case during the course of the thirteenth century. So, for example, the protracted period of tension between Henry III and London in the mid-thirteenth century was sparked off in 1239, and subsequently fuelled by, the king's interference in the election of civic officials. The Londoners' deeply hostile response meant that between 1239 and 1257 the king took the government of the city into his own hands at least ten times.[32]

Difficulties between the Crown and London government were exacerbated at this point, as indeed they were often to be, by other factors: faction-fighting among the elite; the preferential treatment given to alien merchants who proved so financially rewarding to the Crown. Both these additional factors encouraged disorder, and it was issues of public order that were equally likely to provoke tension between the king and individual towns. Both in London and in the regions the king was driven to intervene where a town's ability to govern itself seemed to have broken down. As urban government became more sophisticated in the later middle ages, less drastic channels for the remedy of abuse were put into place, but the Crown was still called on to intervene when local arbitration failed. Acute crisis brought the suspension of London's liberties in the reign of Richard II; Norwich had its liberties suspended in the middle of the fifteenth century and York at the end of the century, because of bitter internal discord.

Sheer lack of documentation makes it impossible to make a similar assessment of the relationship of the Crown to Scottish towns before the fifteenth century, though the very small scale of most of these towns and the concentration of wealth in the four main east-coast towns meant there was less scope for assertions of urban autonomy. Intervention by the Scottish Crown is best documented for the mid-sixteenth century, and is considered below in the context of the agitation of the crafts for better representation.

Royal towns set the agenda for forms of development; seigneurial towns generally achieved far less independence, with borough officers remaining the lord's appointees. It seems to have been ecclesiastical lords who were the most reluctant to accept change and who proved to be the most abrasive in relations with townspeople, though there were some striking exceptions. Neither in Westminster nor Durham was there any evidence of conflict. Nor in the much smaller town of Strat-ford-upon-Avon was there any difficulty between the town and its lord, the Bishop of Worcester.[33] The same is true of many Scottish ecclesiast-ical burghs, though it is rather less safe here to argue from the silence of the records, as that silence is fairly comprehensive.

But tension rather than co-operation does seem to have been more characteristic of English monastic towns, resulting in some spectacular instances of violence, particularly at times of national crisis, for example in 1327, when the government of Edward II was disintegrating. In 1381, at the time of the Peasants' Revolt, the worst urban riots occurred in towns with repressive ecclesiastical lords. Perhaps most notorious were the dismal relations between the town and abbey of Bury St Edmunds, where a guerrilla war was conducted throughout the middle ages. All moves by the town to obtain a measure of independence were resisted tooth and nail; short-term victories – the head of the prior placed on the pillory in the 1381 riots – were followed by long-term defeats, because the power of the Crown was almost always moved in behind the author-ity of the prior. It was only with the dissolution of the monasteries in the sixteenth century that monastic towns could gain a measure of self-government.

However, there was plenty of scope for mutual advantage if the lord worked in co-operation with the leading townsmen, as was the case with Boston, where the lord, the Earl of Richmond, was the protector rather than the despoiler of the urban elite.[34] Other protectors and arbitrators were also sought from among the most potent landholders, not least by towns which had already acquired a measure of independent govern-ment. By the later middle ages this search for good lordship can be found in all parts of the British Isles. The need was most urgent in Ire-land, where the effective abdication of royal authority in the later middle ages left most towns dependent on the defensive patronage of the local nobility. In fact the fiscal privileges granted to Irish towns in the late fifteenth and early sixteenth centuries were not a response to the distressed economies of places such as Waterford and Cork, which were doing rather well, but a recognition of the power of the magnate protectors like the Earls of Ormond and Desmond, that made any dues uncollectable.[35] The power of the Scottish lairds was also formidable, though the assumption of 'total noble domination' is now being reassessed in the light of local circumstances. Aberdeen is probably the most extreme example, a city run by merchant lairds. Aberdeen had also entered into a bond of manrent with the Earls of Huntly in 1453, effectively making the city the retainer of the Earl, but there were other lords to whom it made payments amounting in all to almost half the burgh income in the 1490s.[36] This relationship between town and landed power should not be seen as wholly supine on the part of the town, but is evidence of the growing strength of horizontal bonds in society already referred to, tying the urban elite closely to the country gentry.

*An urban community?*

Despite the vicissitudes stemming from royal financial demands, involvement in national politics, and arguments over jurisdictional boundaries, on balance the relationship of the town with the king and with the most powerful landed interests was not fundamentally destructive but could be negotiated to mutual advantage. But the assumption has been in the foregoing discussion that the town acted as a unified entity and that there was a consensus as to what could and might be achieved. This was not necessarily the case. Within the town, to whom did advantage accrue; was it in fact to the whole urban community or limited to sections of that community; who ran the town, and for whose benefit?

Currently there are two different perspectives on British medieval towns. One, favoured by Reynolds and argued strongly for by Rosser, emphasises the effectiveness of the integration of the various parts of the urban community. To the question posed by Bossy of why 'human communities aren't continuously in a state of disintegration' they respond with an account of the shared assumptions underlying urban government, assumptions based on acceptance of hierarchy and the right of the better sort, the minority of *meliores* to govern the lesser, the majority.[37] This government was not wholly self-interested, because in Britnell's words, 'economic individualism was not a recognised ideal'.[38] The corporatist approach to government meant that regulation was designed to prevent excess profit in trade in order to protect consumers, though the existence of a perception of the necessity of such protection was, as we should well recognise, no kind of bar in reality to the amassing of huge profits, and indeed could even legitimate them, duty having been seen to have been ostensibly done.

As long as reality did not stray completely out of range of the ideal, it is argued that there was general consent for this regime and acceptance of a hierarchically ordered society. Pragmatically, such consent was reinforced by the fact that only the better sort could afford to govern. Tensions existed within the community, but they arose from failures in the way the system was used rather than from fundamental criticisms of the entire structure. Hence tension might arise as the result of faction-fighting between members of the elite. Alternatively, it might mark the complaint of the lesser sort, the *minores*, against maladministration, that is, criticism of individual failure to govern well rather than a criticism of the system as a whole.

An alternative perspective is that argued by Rigby, one that lays far more emphasis on the tensions existing within medieval society and the extent to which such antagonisms were able to force change. Rigby uses the sociological theory of closure to give a framework to the structures of power within medieval society and to examine the meaning of the term 'community'.[39] Communities identify themselves not purely as groups with shared priorities, but crucially by whom they exclude as well as those they include. The terms of inclusion may be very catholic: this may make the town appear a broad-based community where sectional interests were integrated into the interests of the whole. But the whole idea of closure, the definition of a group by exclusion, necessarily entails the privileging of the group in power, and that group may be tacitly far more narrowly constituted than the explicit terms of inclusion imply; there will be an inner circle.

Furthermore, the regimes so constituted may have been accepted as fairly inevitable, but such acceptance might be no more than grudging, and certainly not harmonious. It might entail a criticism of the structure of a government which lacked adequate accountability to the community that it purported to articulate. The dissent of the illiterate is only sporadically recorded; it is characteristic of the 'gossip communities' of the disadvantaged that they do not talk outside their own group, so we seldom see the way the world is constructed by them.[40] It is possible that this world-view emphasises horizontal bonds of society more than the vertical bonds so favoured by those in positions of power. There are elements of truth in both approaches, the harmonious and the confrontational. But ultimately the stress given to one or other of these interpretations of the way that urban society operated will depend on the preoccupations of the individual historian. What should be at issue is the ability of either interpretation to explain how the town worked and the way in which government and society changed over time.

The first thing to establish is who was running the town. Although in theory borough government should have been open to the participation of anyone who was a fully paid-up member of the urban community, in practice it was the leading members of the community, the *maiores*, who monopolised the chief offices. In small towns Hilton suggests that a fairly substantial proportion of those families who became 'established and respectable' constituted a 'reasonably broad elite' made up of small-scale traders and artisans serving as jurors and court officials.[41] In a middling town like Kilkenny, with 119 burgesses in the late fourteenth century, council members and officers would constitute one-fifth of all burgesses at any one time – though of course the burgesses themselves only constituted a minority of townspeople.[42] Larger towns were more socially stratified, with a proportionately smaller elite controlling urban government, though just how small a group it was is something we will return to.

The ruling elite was not entirely made up of townspeople or those involved in commerce; there was always scope for interested outsiders to become involved. Outsiders had a place among the patriciates of twelfth-century English towns. Here the controlling influence in the eleventh and early twelfth centuries was not purely or even dominantly mercantile but included moneyers (who were usually royal officials), other officials of either a seigneurial lord or of the king, officials of the Church, and local landowners, together constituting a class of people generally referred to as *ministeriales*.

From the twelfth century onwards the expansion of the economy led to the growing dominance of urban merchants in English towns, though the landed interest maintained a strong presence in some places such as York and Coventry well into the thirteenth century. As Britnell points out, only when merchants could afford to become sedentary, and not travel with their goods, could they become major players in urban government, a development that required the growth of an 'infrastructure of law and routine' that evolved between the eleventh and thirteenth centuries.[43] So, for example, in early fourteenth-century Northampton there were still four coroners because it was argued that the majority of burgesses were merchants who had to travel, so enough coroners were needed to work a rota.[44] The planted towns of Wales, Scotland and Ireland were specifically intended to foster a profitable trading class, but political considerations meant that, particularly in Wales, there was a prominent stratum of officials, either those of the Crown or those of the marcher lords. And in all towns, with the elaboration of administration and the growth of the legal machine, professionals, particularly lawyers, came to play an increasingly prominent role in urban government by the fifteenth century. The elite was not closed (although the difficulty of getting into it will be considered in the next chapter) and there was room for some unlikely social climbers among the ranks of the *maiores*. It was possible for a small number of Welshmen to hold office within some towns. The same was true for ethnic Irish. Robert of Bree, mayor of Dublin, did particularly well, being native Irish; he was accepted within English law, presumably because of his commercial success.[45]

A judicious marriage was one way in which an outsider could ally himself to the existing *maiores*. Marriage within the civic elite was political, and a network of marriages linking members of the elite was an effective way for the *maiores* to define their social boundaries. But although marriage was one way of reinforcing the networks of interest groups that bound together the elite of medieval towns, alliances alone could not guarantee that members of the elite would maintain their hold on the chief offices of urban government. Much of the recorded trouble in the thirteenth- and early fourteenth-century towns in England was over the issue of which people should be in control and how that control could be used to personal advantage. The exposure of a fraudulent guild in York in the early years of the fourteenth century illustrates most of the critical issues. Andrew de Bolingbroke, one of the *maiores*, along with 53 cronies, set up a religious fraternity in the city, which, far from being purely pious, was acting as a alternative to the legitimate government of the city. The borough courts were ignored by this faction and all possible legal and commercial business was channelled before the officials of the fraternity. Further than this, among the members of the fraternity were a number of the tax assessors of the city, and they took great care to place the main tax burden on the shoulders of non-fraternity members, particularly the poor. A few of them even moved residence to within the boundaries of the ecclesiastical liberties to avoid any unpleasant consequences of their actions.[46] In this episode we have two key ingredients of urban strife: factionalism among the elite and the exploitation of the poor, the two often, as in this case, going hand in hand.

Faction-fighting was certainly prevalent among urban elites and is seen by what might be called the 'holistic' historian as the main cause of urban unrest and the chief means of promoting changes in urban government. Faction-fighting among the elite was clearly instrumental in restructuring the government of London in the thirteenth century. This century saw almost continuous conflict between dynasties whose rivalry was fuelled further by the partisan dealings of the Crown, the king giving support to that party which offered the most substantial financial help. The factions tended to be centred on trade or craft guilds. In London the scale of trading meant that instead of a single guild merchant there were, from the thirteenth century onwards, a series of merchant associations, the goldsmiths, pepperers and drapers, for example, who controlled the city government. In the late thirteenth century the hold these existing associations had on power was challenged by new associations, among them groups of victuallers, particularly the fishmongers, and other crafts such as the ironmongers, who had a major stake in the expanding trade of the city. The aspirations of the new associations were no more overtly popular than those of the men they sought to replace, and, once in power, they were concerned to pull up the drawbridge against any lesser crafts that might try similarly to enhance their power by formal organisation. Equally, once in power the new associations established an internal hierarchy that put power in the hands of the mercantile masters of the association, excluding the rank and file of artisans.

The protracted conflict did result in structural changes to the city's government, changes that recognised new patterns of wealth creation. In a new constitution drawn up in 1319 the franchise was redefined so that it came to be dependent on craft membership. However, wealth was still the defining criterion for access to power in London; it was the use made of the rules as much as the rules themselves that determined the composition of the elite. The new way of defining the franchise was to effect greater control among those who ran the more prosperous crafts rather than, as might seem from first appearance, to democratise access to citizenship.[47]

Partisan government by faction within the elite was extremely unlikely to be good government; indeed the York case shows quite clearly that its intention was unjust and oppressive. Conflict and violence in urban society were very often responses of the poor and the middling sort against the unfair government of the rich. The holistic historians argue that government was attacked only when it was manifestly corrupt, and that it was a change in personnel rather than an overthrowing of existing structures that was sought. In contrast, those historians suspicious of the concept of the harmonious urban community would argue that all government by a restricted elite was likely to be oppressive and that urban conflict was prompted by a desire to make the *maiores* more accountable.

There was certainly plenty of complaint, much of it in the form of petitions to the Crown or produced as a result of crown intervention to suppress disturbance. Reynolds marshals a broad range of evidence from thirteenth-century England to show resentment against fiscal and commercial exploitation by the elite: in Oxford in 1256–57 the complaint was against the engrossment of the profitable fish trade by the most wealthy; in Lincoln in 1267 against fraud on tolls, unfair levies and misuse of the courts by the elite.[48] It seems probable that the abuses that emerged into the public arena were only a small proportion of those that customarily went on at a petty level year in, year out. On the face of it these petitions seem levelled at the abuse of power rather than the structures of power. However, petitions to the Crown were likely to be couched in conservative terms in order to elicit any kind of positive response, and our record of objections and dissent is one tailored to fit the discourse of government. Petitions of this sort do imply some form of concerted action among the *minores*, the lesser sort, though this action might be orchestrated from above by disaffected members of the elite.

The difficulty for the powerless was the lack of any kind of adequate organisational base from which to protest. It was a difficulty that became more acute as the mechanisms for urban government developed in the fourteenth and fifteenth centuries. The increase in the documentation of government makes more readily demonstrable the firm control of the urban elite on the exercise of power, and so on economic privilege. In this context it is not surprising that popular resistance might become identified with the faction-fighting amongst the elite. Members of urban elites who found themselves excluded from power might offer themselves as figureheads of popular resentment for strategic purposes. This, it is argued by Nightingale, was the explanation for the violent disorder in the 'turbulent London of Richard II', when conflicting interests among the merchant elite exploded in the bitter rivalry between Nicholas Brembre and John of Northampton, both of them members of the patriciate.[49] Whereas previous interpretations had emphasised the class element in this conflict, with Northampton leading the protests of the disadvantaged against the entrenched power of Brembre's company, the Grocers, Nightingale's case is that Northampton merely sought personal advantage, using whatever sectional interests he could command to achieve this.

However, the harnessing of popular disaffection by mercantile agit-
ators does not mean that the lesser sort were just catspaws and had no
political agenda of their own. More plausibly, Dobson has argued that
the challenge by the 'communitas', those who perceived themselves as ill
done by stakeholders in urban society, against the mercantile elite, was
'one of the major themes in the constitutional history of the late medieval town'.[50] Occasionally there is evidence of a genuine manifestation of
alternative political ideas on behalf of the lesser sort, as was the case with
the London revolt led by Ralph Holland in the 1440s, which argued the
need for active consent among the governed for the actions and authority of the rulers.[51] But for the most part, with crown authority lined up
behind the elite, should disaffection take a wolfish turn, there was no
vehicle which could give sustained expression for popular demands for
representation.

Hence Rigby argues that the objections of the lesser sort in towns
availed them little in the long term. Urban governments did change in
response to complaints, but these changes seem primarily to have served
to adjust relationships between the various interest groups who jockeyed
for position at the top of the urban social hierarchy. So, for example, the
creation of a new council of 12 in Exeter in 1345 was designed to check
the abuses of the mayor and four stewards. But the personnel of the
council were drawn from the same small group of wealthy merchants
that had held the key civic posts, so that the effect was merely to formal-
ise the existing dominance of this class.[52]

The process of elections, whereby access was gained to urban councils,
was tightened up in the fourteenth and fifteenth centuries. Rigby points
out that whereas English borough charters had been more concerned
with relations between Crown and town in the thirteenth century, by the
later middle ages they were coming to be increasingly concerned with
internal government.[53] Rather than vague commitments to election by
all the community which had characterised earlier arrangements, the
way that the community could express its wishes was being spelt out in
detail because, as the clerk of Colchester recorded, 'many troublez, parlous discordes and inconuenientes haue be founde by experience by
cause of the multitude concurrent to such eleccions, presumyng and
vsurpyng enteresse in the seid eleccions wher in dede they owe noon to
haue'.[54] The restriction of the Colchester electorate from 1430 onwards,
rather than being a new departure, was a normalisation of tacit arrangements that already existed to make sure that only the right people got
elected.

Different procedures for election in other towns also served the same purpose, to give the most powerful offices of mayor and sheriff, and the places on the key councils, to those who were 'one of us'. In London in 1426 creative use was made of the ruling of 1315 that only those summoned could come to elections, to engineer a result that defeated the popular candidate for the mayoralty, Ralph Holland. From the restriction of elections emerged the oligarchic governments of late medieval towns in England, Wales and Ireland, run by a tightly integrated group whose hold on power was not threatened by an electoral process that increasingly served to rubber-stamp preferred candidates for office, and who filled up vacancies in conciliar ranks with their own nominees. The creation of closed corporations, where awkward elections by the citizen body were eliminated, was merely an extension of this process.

Much of the recorded popular agitation of the late fourteenth and fifteenth centuries was directed at trying to control the system of elections, so that at least those who monopolised power could in some measure be made accountable to the rest of the community. This was not just a matter of having good rulers, but adequately policed rulers. The claim of the citizens of Norwich excluded from power that 'every person of the least reputation . . . should have as much authority and power in all the elections and other affairs . . . as the most sufficient persons' speaks of a sense of common responsibility that does not square with the concept of a descending form of government where power was vested in the head, the mercantile elite, and with the burgess artisans settling for being the feet of the commonwealth.[55] John Astyn of Grimsby, who was gaoled for the day for claiming he would not be ruled by the mayor but only by his fellows and equals, certainly had a robust perception of his own political worth.[56] In Exeter Kowaleski found much evidence of resentment among the *minores*, but tellingly suggests that the lack of overt violence stems from the fact that the frustrated ambitions of those excluded from office were mitigated by minor office and minor status afforded to those who did not make it into the ranks of the elite.[57] This encapsulates the problem of resistance, the divided interests of those excluded from power. The principle of divide and rule can be seen operating in the system of craft guilds.

*Craft guilds*

No town in the British Isles (except London) was large enough to sustain the kind of artisanal guild that afforded a platform of opposition to oligarchy that existed in continental cities. Indeed, it was only a minority of towns that had craft guilds at all. Major English towns with no recorded craft organisation before the late fourteenth century include Southampton, Gloucester and Coventry. The larger Scottish towns were establishing some craft guilds by the early sixteenth century. In Dublin most guilds were formed relatively late; glovers and tanners had formed the earliest associations, dating from the twelfth century, but most others, such as the barbers, bakers and shoemakers, emerge as guilds in the fifteenth century.[58] Inevitably, craft guilds were only going to emerge in towns large enough to sustain considerable numbers of artisans in the same or related occupations, and even then conglomerate groups were not unusual. In Edinburgh, for example, the hammermen came to include smiths, pewterers, gold and tin workers and leatherworkers. Even then, far from all artisans were included in guilds; the builders are the most striking example of skilled workers whose terms of employment meant that they were seldom formally organised into craft associations.

The earliest craft guilds in provincial towns seem to have emerged as defensive organisations. In principle the guild merchant had included all those who wished to trade within the town. In practice the extent of exclusion could become marked. In Berwick in 1249, 'in order that no particular congregation of burgesses encroach on the liberty of the general guild all particular guilds are to be dissolved and their property given to the new guild'.[59] However this ruling may not have been as public-spirited as it sounds, for the 'particular guilds' may have been those representing the interests of craftspeople who had formed associations in order to combat the pressure put on them by cloth entrepreneurs. This had certainly been the case in English towns by the late twelfth century, when entire social groups, particularly clothworkers, had been earmarked as unacceptable and excluded from the guild merchant, in the interests of those entrepreneurs who wished to keep a tight grip on cloth manufacture. As a reaction these artisans sought to form their own guilds in self-defence. Weavers and fullers were also excluded from some Scottish guild merchants, though we have no record to say whether these exclusions were ever put into force; they certainly had lapsed later, and, by the fifteenth century, clothworkers are found as members of guilds merchant. In England, other early craft guilds developed among the leatherworkers, who were so numerous and prominent a part of urban industry: shoemakers in Oxford in 1160 and saddlers in York in 1181. At a time when new forms of urban government were being worked out, the creation of these guilds lets us briefly glimpse the aspirations of substantial numbers of artisans who wished their position in urban society to be more clearly articulated. The expectations of the artisans that these guilds would give them protection were over-optimistic, and whatever fraternal support may have been offered by such organisations, the parlous financial state of the weavers' guilds by the early fourteenth century is evidence of the impossible cost for the smaller artisan of buying protection against wholesale traders.

When craft guilds re-emerge into the records in the later fourteenth century they are a different species. It was natural for members of the same occupation to group together for the purposes of mutual support. This meant both the provision of assistance in this world by the regulation of fair employment practices and the distribution of charity, and insurance against an overlong spell in purgatory in the next, through the corporate spiritual good works of the fraternity.[60] But such an organisation need have no public face and never emerge into the record. The high profile of late medieval craft associations derives from the way they were integrated into urban government. Like modern charities, craft associations founded for benevolent reasons could find themselves indispensable as an arm of government policy, grafted into civic administration and closely monitored. This is what happened in the fourteenth and fifteenth centuries, and if there was no suitable organisation in existence the council might create one, as was the case with the Northampton tailors in 1444–45.[61]

The searchers of the craft were the intermediaries between the workforce and the city council, responsible for the maintenance of standards of production and of equitable labour relations. Their regulations were subject to mayoral scrutiny and, if necessary, the mayor and council might 'amende, correct and refourme it and every parcell therof at his pleiser'.[62] The English statute of 1437 that made registration of craft ordinances before the civic authorities compulsory was, as in so many other instances, an example of national legislation reiterating what had been local practice for some time. Such regulations were designed to provide a supervisory system for labour relations and for quality control, objectives with which the members of the craft might readily concur. To say that the city council assumed control over the crafts is not to deny that craft organisations might still provide a satisfactory framework for mutual support and a legitimisation of creditworthiness among its members. But the siphoning-off of the revenues of these associations to the coffers of the council is clear-enough evidence of the extent to which they were under the council's political control. It is more helpful to see craft organisations as vehicles of civic administration than as organisations for industrial protectionism.

There was considerable social differentiation within crafts. This is perhaps most obvious in Scotland, where there were seldom merchant guilds, but instead the leading members of particular craft organisations emerged as an effective urban elite. Those at the top of the pile in their craft association might be on the first rung of a desirable social ladder, the *cursus honorum*, the path through civic office of ascending significance, leading for a few to the dizzy heights of the civic elite. Such a procession emphasises the vertical links in society rather than giving expression to a separate artisanal class. The organisation of work reinforces this vertical perspective. Apprentices and servants did not always remain labourers, but might in time become masters. By involving the craft in the process of civic administration, emphasis could be laid on these vertical ties, thus reducing the potential of craft organisations as vehicles of an oppositional ideology – in contrast to the aspirations of the twelfth-century textile guilds.

The normalisation of the civic role of the craft guilds can be interpreted in the context of other steps taken in the fourteenth and fifteenth centuries to limit access to power to the better sort. Those artisans who did prosper enough to join the inner circles of city government did so as individuals and not as representatives of their craft. As has been noted, medieval councils were not closed to the arrival of outsiders who had made a good deal of money, but in a medieval equivalent of the theory of removable inequalities, the successful aspirant to civic power had to leave his craft behind him. In early sixteenth-century Aberdeen the fleshers (butchers), who were specifically excluded from the merchant guild, as were the dyers and shoemakers, had to renounce their craft if they wanted to trade in the staple goods of hides, skins and wool.[63] As a result the craft, and the vast majority of artisans, remained subordinate and effectively powerless.

Much of the recorded tension associated with crafts was between guilds, jockeying for the supervision of quality control; tanners and shoemakers were on notoriously bad terms in many towns. Does this mean that nothing can be made of the horizontal divisions between artisan crafts and the wholesale merchants? These divisions would become more prominent when the systematic exclusion of the crafts from effective political power was damaging the prospects of individual leading members of the crafts, resulting in an enforced craft solidarity against discrimination. This would seem to have been the case in the late

fifteenth century and early sixteenth century when the changed economy resulted in ascendant occupations that wanted a more effective
voice in government. This voice would be an expression of a new interest group, in contrast to the ascent through the hierarchy made by individuals.

Given the prevailing uncertainty as to the economic health of towns at
the turn of the fifteenth and sixteenth centuries, it seems unwise to be
too assertive as to whether it was crises or changing opportunities that
brought about the pressure for wider representation. The growth of a
mass market in some consumer goods, coupled with the realignment of
international trade in favour of the capitals, may have created circumstances in some provincial towns where substantial artisans felt that not
only did they deserve considerably more active participation in government than they had hitherto enjoyed, but that they now also had a reasonable chance of achieving these aspirations. But even so, for some
crafts wealth would never be enough to let them on to the council, as
they were too socially unacceptable – as the Aberdeen fleshers found out.
The recasting of the York constitution in 1517 after decades of agitation
gave representation to respectable craftspeople such as chandlers and
glaziers, but pointedly ostracised the troublesome tanners and shoemakers.[64] Of the nine craft associations in early sixteenth-century Perth,
the three most prestigious, those of the hammermen, skinners and bax-
ters, tried to restrict the election to the office of bailie to one of their
number.[65] In both these cases the sheer persistence of the aspirants and
the scale of the trouble prompted crown intervention over an extended
period of time, to the advantage of the plaintiff crafts, who could not by
then be excluded.

Because of the way that they had been bound into the urban hierarchy, craft organisations did not lend themselves to the expression of
the tensions between the better sort that governed and the lesser who
served the administration. The implication of the apprentice system and
the vertical bonds that sustained a hierarchy within the crafts was that a
wage labourer could ultimately proceed to being a master. But for an
unknown proportion of men, and of course for virtually all women, such
a progression was not an option; moreover this seems to have been a
proportion that was growing in the later middle ages, though the lack of
evidence for the earlier period precludes certainty. Hence organisations
of wage labourers, apprentices and servants were likely to be more
abrasive critics of existing practices than the guilds of master craftsmen.
In 1286 Walter of Maidstone headed a parliament of carpenters in London

that was pretty combative; London journeymen can also be found forming illegal associations in the second half of the fourteenth century, targeting unfair working practices and low rates of pay.[66] When trouble did break out between masters and servants the intevention of the authorities was not always wholeheartedly on the side of the employer. In the early fifteenth century the piece rates of the shoemakers' servants were raised by York city council, despite the opposition of the master shoemakers.[67] This decision should perhaps not be interpreted as manifesting a particularly enlightened spirit; it may merely reflect the fact that master shoemakers almost never held high civic office, so the council could afford publicly to squash them.

Most difficult to control were the semi-skilled and manual labourers, such as the builders referred to above, who seldom formed themselves into craft groups that could be held accountable for the actions of their members. The threat of informal associations is evident in the presentation of Nicholas Dawber before the Colchester court in 1425, because he 'rules all the other labourers in the town of Colchester, and is accustomed to take an excessive wage against the Statute of labourers etc. and is accustomed to exhort all the rest to do likewise'.[68] Colchester was a moderate-sized town, and what happened there was likely to be replicated elsewhere. Informal networking among artisans was the means whereby job opportunities were quickly advertised among the women woolpackers of Southampton; highly unusually, these women were formed into a guild by the council in the early sixteenth century in order to control the activities of a potentially dangerously independent body of women, and presumably to prevent the emergence of a female equivalent of Nicholas Dawber.[69]

An argument has been presented for the consolidation of power in the hands of a small elite, which by the fifteenth century had control over an increasingly elaborate urban government in the larger towns. Was that control worth while? It has been suggested that there was a lack of enthusiasm for taking up civic office by the late fifteenth century. Given the extent of the responsibilities involved, high civic office was a time-consuming and potentially expensive matter, only realistically open to those who could afford to delegate their money-making concerns to others. It was not only the elaboration of business that put pressure on urban finances; status itself was costly, as it came to be wrapped in layers of elaborate pomp. Urban officials were personally responsible for any deficits incurred during their periods of office. If the town's finances were in a particularly parlous state, anyone taking office would be guaranteed to end up with some loss; for some the dignity was not worth the price.

However, too much should not be made of the 'flight from office'. It may even be that nominating ineligible individuals to serve as officials was a disguised form of taxation; their inevitable refusal of the honour made them liable to a fine. As with the entire debate about the decline of towns, generalisation is rather dangerous. Some towns were clearly putting in effective special pleading when it came to poverty: by the 1520s Dublin and Drogheda were complaining bitterly that Cork, Waterford and Limerick paid next to nothing to the Crown, so that 'every man [was] striving to be mayor or ruler for the great profit to be received to their own use'.[70] The elaborate pomp and closed governments of late medieval towns may have encouraged some men to migrate to smaller, less closely-regulated towns. On the other hand, the pomp demonstrated the status of and recognition due to the urban elite as part of the national political community, exercising extensive powers of jurisdiction on behalf of the Crown.

### The Town in the Kingdom

Integration of the urban community in the wider political community was made explicit in the summoning of burgess representatives to parliament. In reality the single most important reason for towns to be represented in parliament was taxation. The summoning of burgesses was a tactic devised to diffuse opposition from a sector that offered rich pickings to a needy treasury. Here there is a marked difference between England on one hand and the experiences of Wales, Scotland and Ireland on the other. Wales and Ireland can be dealt with the most concisely. Welsh boroughs had no representation in the English parliament; their acquiescence in taxation was assumed and not invited. In Ireland parliament had little independence, being subject almost completely to the royal council. Representatives from ten boroughs were meant to be sent to the Irish parliament from the fourteenth century onwards, but only towns in the area around Dublin were represented regularly. By the fifteenth century, in any case, decisions made in Dublin had little relevance for towns on the west and south coasts for whom effective power lay with local lords.

The Crown's relations with towns in Scotland was shaped by the fact that they were extremely lightly taxed. The Scottish government, not committed either to the radical centralising of the English administration or to massive military campaigns, was able for the most part to live off its own resources, revenues from land, supplemented by revenues from customs, rather than by levying direct taxation. The levies that did exist obviously touched those living in royal towns, in the form of the farm and in duties on overseas trade. But direct taxation was levied very rarely and only in periods of acute crisis, as, for example, with the capture and ransom demand for King David II in 1357. The urgent and exceptional need for cash to meet this demand meant that new ways had to be found for raising money, and the Crown was forced to consult with representatives from the towns on just how this was to be raised. Although town burgesses had been summoned to parliament in Scotland in the early fourteenth century, they only came regularly after 1357, sitting with the clergy and the barons in one joint session. Unhappily for the historian, the towns on this and subsequent occasions compacted to pay tax in the form of a lump sum from all the towns together, so we can have no knowledge of the distribution of the burden either between or within towns.

The burgesses from some English towns also came to be included in parliament from the late thirteenth century onwards. England and Wales were far more heavily taxed than Scotland, and not surprisingly, just how this money was to be extracted caused tensions, not just between the Crown and the towns, but, as seen above, more acutely within towns, over the extent to which the tax burden was unfairly distributed.

Anglo-Norman kings had the right to demand money from those living within the royal demesne, that is, on land in the king's hand, including royal towns. But these levies, known as aids or tallages, were neither regular or universal. Extra funds might also be raised from towns through the sale of privileges and the granting of liberties, but these were more in the nature of a windfall tax. What was sought was a regular way of demanding money. During the thirteenth and early fourteenth centuries two particularly lucrative devices were developed: direct taxation based on an assessment of the value of movable goods, and customs on imports and exports.

The turning point in the development of these taxes came in the 1290s, when Edward I's military campaigns created an unprecedented demand for money. But the hiking of rates to extraordinary levels raised the issue of just whose 'consent and counsel' was going to commit the community of the realm to this expense. Consent and counsel had largely been a baronial prerogative, but the scale of demands by Edward I and subsequently by Edward III meant a wider representation was needed. Some consultation with various interest groups was tried: agreement was obtained from specifically merchant assemblies for some of the duties on trade, but the heavyweights among merchants did not always speak either for the smaller merchants or for all towns. The solution lay in the gradual evolution of parliament during the course of the four-teenth century as the vehicle whereby those likely to make the most diffi-culties about taxation could be consulted and cajoled into granting it. Representatives of towns were invited to sit with country representatives as spokesmen for the community of the realm from the 1270s onwards; by the 1330s the presence of the towns had become accepted practice. By the late fourteenth century the principle had been established that the consent of the gentry and townsmen sitting together in the commons, and distinct from the baronial representatives in the lords, was necessary for any grant of direct taxation and for the renewal of grants of customs and exports.

The list of towns that had a voice in this process only stabilised in the course of the fourteenth century. When summonses to attend parlia-ment went out to the towns in the late thirteenth century, they were issued by the sheriff. Sheriffs changed their minds over time as to which towns should be represented and they adopted different procedures for summoning representatives, and it is this that accounts for the unbal-anced distribution of parliamentary boroughs, with an undue number located in the south and south-west, an imbalance that became fossilised in the following century. Not all those towns which returned MPs were in fact boroughs: for example, Southwark, with its complex government of five manors, was treated as a town for the purposes of representation and returned two MPs.[71] Nor, perversely, did all those places deemed to be towns for the purposes of taxation have MPs. When taxes on movable goods were raised, they were levied at different rates for town and coun-try. This was usually a tenth of the value of movables for the townspeople and a fifteenth for country dwellers, a differential arising most probably because it was easier to coerce towns into paying more. The decision as to which communities were to be taxed as towns was taken in the light of custom, but was open to variation.

The commons as a whole were not particularly representative of the community of the realm, but rather of the property owners; equally, urban MPs were not so much representative of the town as of the interest groups which ran the town. The process by which urban MPs were elected is little known, but contests were rare. The job was monopolised by the elite or, increasingly, their allies among the rural gentry. By 1450, 50 per cent of boroughs had non-resident MPs; by the early sixteenth century it was 70 per cent. However, this should not be seen as a predatory invasion of borough freedoms by rural interlopers, but the expression of a community of interest between the leading townsmen and the rural gentry; it was the gentry who played the dominant role in the commons and were a useful asset to the towns. Quite what the townsmen did in parliament themselves is a bit of a mystery, as they do not figure largely in the surviving record of proceedings.

The priority for members of the commons was to keep the tax burden on the propertied classes as low as possible. Taxes on movables, though easy to assess and collect, did not touch the serious wealth of land or incomes. Up until 1334 the levies on movables were at least reassessed on each occasion that the tax was granted, but from that date on the amount paid by each community, including each town, was fixed. Given the changes to the economy in the late fourteenth and fifteenth centuries, the relationship of this sum to real wealth became more and more remote. Such experiments as were made to exploit the true levels of wealth were neither impartial or realistic, as they were designed not to hurt the parliamentary class: the poll taxes of 1377–81 are an example of a failed attempt on the part of the commons to spread the tax burden more widely among the poor. No effective reassessment of wealth for taxation was made until 1513: the stonewalling of the towns and their gentry allies was resoundingly successful for most of the later middle ages.

This chapter began by asking how distinct urban communities were legally and administratively. Once again the answer has to depend on time and place. Towns within the British Isles were conceived of as part of the royal machinery for justice and administration, however devolved the delivery of these might be. But although the underlying perception of the role of the town applied equally to Cork, Carlisle or Aberdeen, inevitably, because of the divergent political experience of the different parts of the British Isles, towns developed in markedly different ways. Despite the privileges they had, or strove to acquire, despite the variety of individual custom, the legal framework of English towns did not mark them out as fundamentally different to rural society. The same common law applied to rural and urban communities. Equally, in Scotland, where boroughs were introduced along with military feudalism, there were no substantive differences between the law of the burghs and the general

law of the land. English towns were certainly far more elaborately governed than Scottish by the fifteenth century, but it was an elaboration
that went hand in hand with the centralising powers of the Crown, a
centralisation that did not begin to happen in Scotland until the later
fifteenth century. The power of the urban oligarchies who controlled
late medieval English towns was rooted in delegated authority; the interests of the urban elite closely bound up with those of the Crown. The
ranks of the oligarchs were filling up with lawyers; their social ties were
with the rural gentry who shared their role.

Welsh towns were even more explicitly agents of government. Far
more were planted than were economically necessary, and within them
the crown presence was very obvious in administrative as well as military
terms. They were distinguished from the rural areas, where Welsh law
prevailed well into the fifteenth century. Racial division was further consciously underlined by the marked discrimination in favour of English
burgesses in the later middle ages. The English response to the revolt of
Owain Glyn Dŵr only exacerbated this discrimination, but a less obvious
result of the dislocation caused by the revolt was to accelerate the move
away from Welsh law and custom in rural areas. And because law is a
crucial factor in shaping the identity of a community, the move towards
English law arguably would ultimately contribute towards making the
urban cuckoos seem less alien in their Welsh nests. In Ireland the process worked in the opposite way. Small towns came to be absorbed back
into Gaelic society. Larger towns became islands of English law. Their
distinction from the Gaelic law of the surrounding countryside, and the
necessity for burgesses to adopt Gaelic law when dealing with the Irish,
were a measure of the failure of colonisation.

# 4

## URBAN SOCIETY

The environment in which people lives shapes the way they behave, so the questions this chapter seeks to address relate to how distinctive the social and cultural environment was in the medieval town. Did towns give rise to new social forms and new ideas? Were they as civilising as Archbishop Pecham considered them to be?

### Urban Topography

One fundamental influence on the way a society operates is its built environment. Although elements of the countryside intruded into the town in the form of orchards and gardens, physically the town was distinct. Central to each town was the exchange of goods in the market place and to a large extent, urban topography served to underline this purpose. Even the most ostentatious urban building projects, the construction of walls and gates, were as much statements defining the privileged economic community that constituted the town as they were defensive. As we have already noticed, towns did not always build walls, and where they were built, progress on construction might be very slow.

Administrative buildings were located near the market or in other key commercial sites such as bridge crossings; York city council built themselves a chamber on Ouse Bridge itself. Although town courts and guilds merchant needed, from their inception, somewhere to meet and deliberate, there was initially no necessity for these assemblies to be in a dedicated building and larger public meetings generally took place outdoors. However, with the elaboration of urban government, a fixed site to accommodate both the growing body of business and records, and the burgeoning sense of dignity of civic officials, became desirable. In Scotland the various purposes of government were served by the tollbooth, documented from the later thirteenth century, and functioning as town hall, court house and prison, and located either on the edge of the market place or on an island within it.[1] English towns were not served by quite such multi-purpose buildings. Council chamber and prison were distinct; the guild merchant might have built a separate hall for its own deliberations. In the later middle ages other sectional interests in the larger towns, religious guilds or even the richest crafts were building themselves halls, but even at this late date, meetings more characteristically took place within religious houses, churches or chapels, or within the large houses of men of influence. Towns, and particularly small towns, were not necessarily distinguished by impressive public or corporate buildings.

It was the streetscapes of towns which made up the most distinctive feature of urban topography, dictated by the commerce that was the town's *raison d'être*. Urban properties were packed in close together, the characteristic burgage tenement having a short frontage on to the main road with a long backland, an arrangement that made it possible to fit in as many units as possible along the busiest streets. The basis of this building pattern was already in place in the larger English towns such as London and Lincoln in the eleventh century, and was replicated as towns grew or were founded throughout the British Isles. So, for example, there was a basic similarity between burgage plots laid out in Perth, varying between 18 and 29 feet in width and those in Kilkenny or New Ross, where the town's foundation charters specified a width of 20 feet for a burgage.[2] The length of a burgage plot varied much more, and depended on the particular circumstances of urban growth. No town, however consciously planted, followed an ideal plan with consistent and wholly regular plot sizes; all responded to some extent to existing topographical features, whether those were streets already in place or even, as in the case of Lichfield, field boundaries.[3] Town plan analysis, a technique used by urban historical geographers to unpick the stages of urban development, has demonstrated that no clear distinction can be made in this respect between planned and organic towns. Both evolved in a way that accommodated existing conditions and responded to local patterns of exchange.

When there was pressure on building space, speculators were encouraged to subdivide existing properties into even smaller shops and dwellings, but the pattern of such speculation again depended on local conditions. Subdivision was at its height in the early fourteenth century, whereas in the later middle ages falling populations often meant the amalgamation of plots, wasted holdings and empty tenements – and presumably more individual square footage for the remaining inhabitants. However, this was not always the case: prime city property was still at a premium in some fifteenth-century towns, for example in Westminster, where subdivision of properties continued apace. The problem of space seems to have been resolved somewhat differently in Scotland by the still mysterious development of the tenement building, which had made its appearance by the fifteenth century.

In the less desirable back streets of the town, cheap one-storey housing spread out along the roads. The same sort of building tended to characterise the suburbs that trailed along the roads leading into towns. Suburbs had more open space than the town proper and potentially offered scope to institutions or individuals with the money to be more expansive in their building. But suburbs were not generally favoured, for they tended to house the poorer elements of the urban community, or else crafts such as that of the tanners that made smelly and unappealing neighbours.

The congestion of urban living fuelled the preoccupation of urban authorities with building regulations, problems of refuse disposal, sanitation and water supplies. Most buildings were timber-framed, and though straw thatching was banned in London from the early thirteenth century, it persisted in provincial towns until much later. Hence there was also the ever-present threat of fire, exacerbated by the fact that bakehouses, foundries and smithies existed in the heart of the built-up area. It was, however, deliberate arson, and not an industrial accident, that caused Carlisle to burn down in 1292: one Simon of Orton had been disinherited and, enraged, he set fire to the house he claimed was his, destroying much of the town as a result.[4]

### Households

Congestion rendered privacy a rarity. Domestic accommodation, the workshop and shop generally shared the same premises. This served to underline the fact that the basic social unit within the town was the household; but saying this is easier than defining what the word 'household' means. Because the contemporary record keepers were only interested in the legal and fiscal responsibilities and obligations of the head of household, we cannot be sure about how this most fundamental social institution was constituted. Most of the evidence is English, late and flawed. Even the most comprehensive lists of personnel drawn up for taxation purposes, the English poll taxes of the late fourteenth century, excluded juveniles. Other evidence can be used to flesh out the picture of the urban household, particularly wills, though these notoriously often do not even include all members of the immediate family such as sons and daughters, let alone remoter relations or live-in servants. There is also a danger in extrapolating back conclusions drawn from wills that become more abundant in the late fifteenth and early sixteenth centuries. Equally, testamentary evidence will give insights into the family structure of the rich, but not that of the poor.

What can be said for certain is that households were overwhelmingly led by men; female heads of household were a minority, usually widows. Marriage was the norm, the social ideal for men and women; for women this meant substituting subordination to her husband for that she had owed to her father. Gender historians have drawn attention to the fundamental importance of the domestic unit in defining the nature of medieval patriarchy.[5] Women in urban society had considerable economic and legal freedom outside and to some extent inside marriage. Politically they were powerless, a powerlessness that, to a large extent, vitiated their legal rights. The political began with the domestic, and the public authority of men was an extension of the authority they wielded as heads of households. There were no viable social roles for women outside the household save for those limited opportunities offered by the Church. This is not to say that married townswomen were passive, acquiescent and subservient. The life story of Margery Kempe shows the determined and inventive use made of the possibilities open to a fourteenth-century townswoman.[6] After a series of business enterprises, 20 years of marriage and 14 children, Margery finally bribed her husband into a mutual vow of chastity, by paying his debts, so that she could pursue her own spirituality, a path she followed with considerable courage and endurance, sometimes with her husband in tow to support her. What does remain something of an issue is how far gender alone defined women's position. The experience of a wife of a dauber or paver was going to be fundamentally different to that of the wife of even a moderately rich merchant, as Margery was. But however wide the gulf in material conditions, in the end the ideology which defined women as subordinate within the household constrained their lives outside the household, and almost always excluded them from public positions of responsibility.

By the later middle ages the urban household ideally comprised the nuclear family of husband, wife, minors and one or more servants, depending on the degree of affluence. When the transformation away from larger kin-based households took place is still a matter of debate. Nor is there much certainty about the age when marriage took place. There is an ongoing debate on whether late medieval townspeople married in their teens, or whether by then there had been a shift to the pattern characteristic of the sixteenth century, when men and women contracted what is termed 'late companionate marriages', that is, where both parties were in their twenties.[7] It is probably a mistake to generalise too confidently as there are marked regional differences in the way that population changed. In particular, economic conditions in one place that made early marriage possible may not have been replicated in another. Two factors in particular may have meant that urban marriage patterns differed to those in rural areas. First there was an imbalance of the sexes in towns; in very general terms this was in the order of 100 women to 90 men.[8] This would restrict marriage options, but as will be seen, it most probably worked to the disadvantage of older widows. Second, it may also be that the prospects of employment for women as servants in late medieval towns persuaded them to postpone marriage, though this is not an argument that carries weight with those historians who see the majority of late medieval towns as faced with economic crisis. There is also the difficulty that at those times and in those places when the urban economy was expanding, with more jobs being available for women, there seems to be less reason for them to postpone marriage for what might be the rather unenviable conditions of a long-term servant contract.

This takes us to the question of how many children women had in their care. To some extent the options for work open to married women were constrained by the amount of time they devoted to the bearing and raising of children. Late marriage meant fewer children, but equally the size of the sibling group would, brutally, depend on how many of the children survived. It seems tragically certain that Margery Kempe lost most of her 14 children in their infancy (though neither her silence on the subject or, more generally, the prevalence of infant mortality, can be used to argue that children were not mourned when they died young). On family size, the consensus at present is that urban populations did not reproduce themselves; even among the wealthiest families it was usually only two or three children who survived into adolescence in the later middle ages. Early sixteenth-century evidence from Coventry shows that the average size of sibling groups for artisans was under two.[9]

There were surprising differences between towns as to when adult-
hood was deemed to have been reached; in Southampton it was 14, in
Bristol, 21. These differences have yet to be explained, as has their significance. It is generally assumed that boys might leave home to go into
training between the ages of 12 and 16, but this does not reveal much
about their training before this age or, of course, about the training of
girls, either in domestic duties or craft skills. It seems to have been
unusual for adult offspring to live with either parents or siblings, though
there is a certain amount of difficulty in reconciling the scanty evidence
of household structure with legal rulings about the place of a widow after
her husband's death. Scottish widows were by custom allowed possession of the inner part of the matrimonial house, which suggests the possibility of live-in grannies. Similarly, urban custom in England gave the
widow terms in the main tenement of her husband for at least a year
after his death. In the event of her not marrying again, some form of
accommodation would have to have been arranged with any surviving
adult children. But most widows did not marry again, and whatever
forms of accommodation were reached with children, it was still the case
that widows were amongst the most vulnerable people in medieval
towns. A large proportion of the marginals living in or on the edge of
poverty in the most undesirable tenements were likely to be widows.
When statistics become available, as in early sixteenth-century Coventry,
they are startling: there were nearly nine times as many widows heading
households as there were widowers; over half of them lived completely
alone, with no servants or children.[10]

Live-in servants were an important component of the English medieval household, and it seems reasonable to extend that supposition to
the other parts of the British Isles that were urbanised, where economic
organisation closely paralleled that of England. Servants were a 'palp-
able expression of a householder's status', and even in a time of crisis, as
in early sixteenth-century Coventry, nearly 40 per cent of households
had servants. In contrast, Southwark, itself a suburb of London and not
a prestigious place to live, only 19 per cent of households listed in the
1381 poll tax had servants. However, even where servants were most
abundant, it was unusual for any household to employ more than two at
any one time, and only the very wealthiest men (and occasionally women)
could afford to support households of up to four or more servants.[11]

The mean size for late medieval urban households, taking all these
factors into account, has been calculated at some 4 to 4.5 people. But
such mean sizes homogenise experience, and hide the differences between

the expectations of men and women, and those of men of different occupations. They tend also to hide the changing composition of the urban household, the introduction of step-parents and step siblings being the inevitable result of high mortality.

High mortality rates also meant that the urban population as a whole was very fluid. Towns probably had to rely on immigration just to sustain their populations, let alone grow. Small towns drew on local villages within a radius of about five miles, and successful burgesses of these small towns hopefully went on to prosper in larger regional centres. Regional centres recruited from an area of 20 miles, perhaps 40 for a city like Bristol, and the capitals attracted immigrants from much further afield, London drawing people from all over the British Isles. The plantation of towns and colonisation produced a massive population movement; Scottish towns filled up with Flemings, Welsh towns were populated from the West Midlands and the West Country, Irish towns from the marches, the West Country and Wales.

Many of these migrants, particularly those moving over a short distance, must have had local contacts that they could utilise to find lodgings. Girls and boys were placed in urban families for training and apprenticeship by means of formal contract, or as was more often probably the case, by informal arrangement. Opportunists would simply arrive to try their luck, picking up contacts at the alehouse. We catch the unlucky, and the more unattractive, in legal records: Nicholas Wodhill, 'alias Nicholas Leche late of London, alias of York, leche', was given a general pardon in 1440 and a specific pardon for the rape of the daughter of a York vintner; the entry conjures up the image of a glib-tongued quack who moved on when conditions got too hot.[12] Medieval townspeople were generally suspicious of any unvouched-for incomers, who might have the potential to damage the economic prospects of those who considered themselves to be stakeholders in the urban community.

Foreigners included anyone from another district, whereas aliens were those from another state, including, of course, the English in Scotland and the Scots in England. Probably less than one per cent of the population in England in the later middle ages was alien, but those aliens were clustered in London and the ports. Their presence was far more noticeable therefore in English towns than in the country, and by analogy the same was probably the case elsewhere in the British Isles. Aliens who worked as servants would perforce be scattered through the town, but where numbers made it feasible the more independent artisans and traders congregated in particular streets, as, for example, the Dutch immigrants on the east side of King Street in Westminster.[13]

Did the distribution of housing underline or reinforce social divisions between other sections of the population? It seems likely that there was a considerable amount of physical mobility within towns because the majority of properties were rented by the later middle ages. Keene's study of London reveals a restless population who changed tenancies regularly, though small-town dwellers may not have exhibited the same degree of movement.[14] Despite this restlessness there was a certain amount of zoning in medieval towns. As we have seen, the homes of single people and widows tended to be clustered in the suburbs or poorer parts of the town. The refreshment of businessmen, professionals and travellers meant a concentration of sellers of food and drink in the centre of towns: King Street, Westminster was positively awash with drinking houses.[15] But service industries like these, and tailors and shoemakers, were also scattered throughout the town. Some industries had specifications that encouraged clustering: Durham tanners' deeds, for example, frequently stipulated the right to a watercourse.[16] Merchants' houses were found in the commercially significant city centre, but not to the exclusion of poorer properties that were shoehorned in beside or behind them, documentary evidence from English towns being paralleled on this point by archaeological evidence from Scotland. The most physically distinct sectors of urban society were those clergy in communities bound by a rule where a physical wall symbolised the divide of clerical and lay, though a fair amount of individual leaping over that wall on illicit visits of pleasure made the divide more ideological than practical. Different sectors of the lay urban community cannot therefore be said usually to have been always clearly physically divided. However, what remains to be seen is whether physical proximity meant the same thing as a sense of community.


## Wealth and Social Mobility

Wealth was the basis of status within medieval towns, although there were some prejudices that money could not eradicate. The Jews were among the wealthiest inhabitants of twelfth- and early thirteenth-century English towns, protected for the financial services they provided for the Crown, but never socially integrated, and from the late twelfth century onwards subject to growing anti-Semitism until their expulsion by

Edward I in 1290. Racial discrimination operated against other groups, though, as we have seen, the wealthy Irish or Welsh could buy their way into urban society in the long run. Other prejudices were social rather than racial, a dislike of hands-on, dirty or smelly work, as with that of butchers or tanners, a dislike exacerbated by the fact that it was sometimes possible for the practitioners of these two crafts to make enough money to buy their way into positions of power.

Any generalisations about the way that wealth and status were distributed in the medieval town have to be hedged with a great many reservations. Obviously the larger the town, the more complex the society, and the more nuanced the levels of the urban hierarchy. Changes in the economy brought social groups into different relationships with each other: the expansion of the economy in the twelfth and thirteenth centuries meant the growth of an increasingly wealthy and self-conscious merchant class that gradually took over the most powerful positions in urban government from the landowners and officials who had previously been most prominent. But, as we saw earlier, there was not always a clear division between merchant and artisan, especially in small towns. Victuallers in particular straddled both groups, and were the very category of artisan likely to profit most from increased standards of living in the later middle ages. The constant re-enactment of sumptuary legislation in the fifteenth century shows the acuteness of both the sense of hierarchy and the extent to which it appeared to be being challenged by prosperous artisans. Finally, the later middle ages saw the emergence of professionals, particularly lawyers, limited in numbers but by virtue of their incomes a significant presence among the elite. As we have seen, this was a development more particularly of England and Wales, for in Scotland the absence of central courts before the fifteenth century meant that a legal profession was very late in developing. What follows, therefore, has to be a very broad-brush consideration of the main divisions in urban society, one which has to be constantly modified when considering individual examples.

The tentative nature of the conclusions is underlined by the nature of the evidence. Estimates of the wealth and status of townspeople have to be pieced together from a variety of sources, with tax records, records of debt, customs accounts and inventories being some of the most fruitful. Inevitably this evidence is heavily biased towards England in the later middle ages, where it is more abundant than it is in Scotland, Ireland or Wales. Both archaeology and the analysis of urban topography can help fill in some of the gaps in our understanding of lifestyles, and of the kind of public and private space available to people at different levels of urban society. Here again there are limitations to the evidence: the flexibility of usage possible in the timber-framed houses that made up the bulk of the urban housing stock leaves little trace in the archaeological record. Equally, the archaeological evidence may be very unrepresentative. The picture of the built environment that has emerged from the excavation of Scottish medieval towns so far is fairly unpromising, construction techniques being on the whole pretty basic, but this may be as result of the fact that excavations have taken place in what were probably the least commercially significant areas.

The majority of town dwellers were poor. Right at the bottom of the social pile was a broad category including the sick and elderly, vagrants and beggars, prostitutes, widows and underemployed or unemployed labourers. Any estimate of the proportion of the population who made up this sector of the very poor is basically guesswork. For most of the middle ages we can only have an impression of the scale of poverty, for example from the overcrowding of pre-plague towns or from the response to charitable doles. The distribution of money, food and clothes at the funerals of the wealthy attracted huge numbers of the poor, estimated at up to 15 000 in early fourteenth-century Westminster. The scale of need that was thus partially addressed is shockingly evident on the occasion of the anniversary of the death of a wealthy London fishmonger in 1322, when alms were given at the gate of the Dominican Friary in Ludgate and the size of the crowd led to 52 people being crushed to death.[17]

One way in which historians try to get access to the number of marginals is by estimating how many people were deemed to be too poor to be taxed. In the post-Black Death period this may have amounted to 25 per cent of the urban population. But exemption from taxation is not a wholly reliable guide. The survey of the late medieval economy made in Chapter 2 showed some towns to be far more exposed to fluctuations in the availability of work and to recession than others. And appalling crises could hit even the most apparently prosperous towns. In such crises those who might be exempted from tax were not necessarily total paupers; they may have been people who who had fallen temporarily on hard times. Phythian-Adams's survey of Coventry census material in the crisis of 1523 shows that, on this occasion, some people with nil tax assessments were living in houses with servants, and so quite clearly not to be classed among the permanent marginals.[18]

Above the very poor was a wide band of people on low or at best modest incomes, but with enough resources to be liable for taxation. Indications are that in the early fourteenth century this broad category encompassed the entire taxable population of small towns; for example, in 1319 the richest man in Bridport was assessed at having possessions calculated for the purposes of taxation at £4 8s.[19] Even in larger towns it was usual for up to 80 to 90 per cent of townspeople to fall into the same general category when it came to taxation, a category that included a wide range of occupations, petty merchants as well as artisans.

Whereas we can only make the very broadest generalisations about the 'middling sort' for the thirteenth and early fourteenth centuries, by the later middle ages it is possible to be a bit more discriminating about the differentials in wealth among those who were taxed. And for the early sixteenth century the English lay subsidies of 1524–25 offer the first opportunity of calculating relative levels of income within urban populations. No direct comparisons between these subsidies and earlier assessments are possible, not only because the basis on which the tax had been levied was different, but also because of the changes to incomes and prices that had occurred in the 150 years since the Black Death. But a similar very broad base to the urban pyramid is still evident. The two lowest tax brackets in these subsidies dealt with people whose goods or annual wages as assessed for tax purposes amounted to less than £5; into these two brackets fell about 70 per cent of the taxable population.[20] These would be men and women in receipt of low pay, or skilled workers in irregular employment; the category might also include apprentices and servants who would hope to be upwardly mobile, and who might subsequently hope to figure in a higher tax bracket.

Above these people whose incomes were at best modest, there was by the later middle ages a category which has, with a lame but unavoidable lack of clarity, to be called the moderately comfortably off. It included skilled artisans in full employment, men who could reckon on an annual income of some £5–£7 by the fifteenth century, to which should be added any additional income from other members of the household. The most prosperous artisans would be bringing in considerably more than this, and even rather more than the small-scale merchants, who also fall into the same category. Into this category also go minor professionals such as stipendiary clergy, or the rectors of poorly endowed urban parishes, who could expect incomes of between £5 and £10 a year. It would be a mistake to regard this as a homogenous group; it was one alert to internal hierarchies. Though there were always exceptions, amongst skilled artisans builders and shoemakers were the least likely to get into this tax bracket; at the top of the pile, considerably better off and merging into the mercantile elite were goldsmiths, vintners and dyers, craftspeople distinguished by the value of their materials or the scope they offered for long-distance trade. A new and upwardly mobile group in this category were the pewterers, who profited from the more general rise in living standards in the later middle ages. Their product, marketed from the fourteenth century onwards, was substantial, showy, but not outrageously expensive, a substitute for silver, and the evidence of inventories shows it displayed in more and more of the homes of the middling rank by the early sixteenth century. Butchers who put meat on the pewter plates were another group likely to profit when living standards rose.

Amongst the middling sort consumer durables were more varied by the fifteenth century than they had been in the thirteenth. Decent quality cooking utensils, clothes and adequate bedding were priorities, multiplying in number with increasing affluence. The inventory of Thomas Bakar, a York stringer (maker of bowstrings) who died in 1436, is characteristic of a skilled but not particularly successful artisan, someone who in terms of the rough categorisation of urban society given above could be accounted 'modestly' rather than 'comfortably' off. Thomas probably lived in a house built on two storeys with small rooms, for his inventory shows a dwelling with a hall, chamber, kitchen and shop. His goods, worth £6 11d in all, conform to expectations: in the chamber he had three beds, one with a tester and hangings, four pairs of sheets, two coverlets and a bolster. His day-to-day utensils were supplemented with 2s' worth of pewter pots. Soft furnishings and painted hangings decorated his hall, none of them worth much on the second-hand market. He owned a sword, bow and arrows and a battleaxe, all of little value, possibly souvenirs of an exciting youth, when he himself pulled bows, rather than just making the strings for them. But Thomas had debts to the tune of £5 3s 2d, including 20s owed for rent on his house and £1 10s 10d for funeral expenses and legacies, and no cash reserves at all were mentioned in his inventory.[21] It is all too easy to see how his wife Alice, one of his two executors, would slide into poverty, selling off his goods to meet his obligations.

By the fifteenth century in England, skilled urban artisans in regular employment could expect to live in a timber-framed house, chimneyed and plastered for warmth, and surrounded by a reasonable collection of creature comforts. To apply the term 'golden age' to these material conditions may be a bit of a hyperbole; but despite the questioning of the more pessimistic historians as to how far this golden age could possibly last into the recession of the mid-fifteenth century, there does seem to be very good evidence for assuming a general rise in the standards of living for the majority of the middling sort of town dwellers in the later middle ages. Direct comparisons on wages and prices are more difficult to make with Scotland after 1367, when Scotland left the sterling standard, but there too, recent indications are that for the majority living standards were rather better by the late fourteenth century than they had been in the late thirteenth.

So much for the middling sort. The truly affluent, the elite of urban society, were always a tiny minority, and generally only to be found in towns where there was long-distance trade. For Kowaleski, investigating wealth distribution in late medieval Exeter, in terms of wealth 'the gap that separated the merchants from other occupations was actually a chasm'.[22] Again, it is not until the lay subsidies of the early sixteenth century that the scale of the wealth of this minority can be quantified. Not untypical of large towns was Norwich, where 2 per cent of the population owned 40 per cent of the taxable wealth. Much of the time this wealth was concentrated in the hands of a few exceptionally rich families. So, for example, William Wigston paid a quarter of the total tax bill for Leicester; equally, in Lavenham, a new boom town of the later middle ages, the Spring family were responsible for 30 per cent of the tax bill.[23] The difficulty of course lies in relating all this very late evidence to English towns before the sixteenth century and to towns elsewhere in the British Isles. But such evidence as there is suggests that it was always the case that in any one locality a very few individuals tended to dominate financially. Though for Scotland there is no statistical base for calculating the wealth of merchants, the moral condemnation of the poet William Dunbar in the fifteenth century is indicative that there was a sharply perceived and unpleasant gulf between the fortunes of rich merchants and the scanty resources of the majority.[24]

The large houses of the rich punctuated the civic streets: performances of the York mystery plays were to take place 'before the house once belonging to John Gisburn, ... Henry Wyman, ... Adam del Bryg', men by then gone, but who had stamped their presence abundantly on civic life.[25] The most affluent aspired to courtyard houses similar to those of the nobility and higher clergy; the luxurious houses of rich ecclesiastics in late medieval Edinburgh are a long way from the rough cottages excavated in Perth. For the greatest merchants it was often still necessary for the street frontage to be given over to commerce, with domestic and storage facilities being located at the back of the courtyard. The disposition of domestic space, even in the largest houses, left little room for privacy. Preference seems to have been as much for an additional parlour as additional bedchambers until the end of the fifteenth century. But the houses of the elite were, of course, furnished with a great deal of lavishness. Money was not poured into furniture, rather it was spent on silver and expensive fabrics, embroidered with intricate and vivid designs: 'in house after house', wrote Thrupp of fourteenth-century London: 'merchants and their families sank to sleep among fantastic visions of dragons, boars' heads, unicorns or sleeping dolphins'.[26]

There is general agreement that the source of wealth that paid for all this luxury was commercial rather than derived from real estate. But it is a great deal easier to assert that money was made in trade than to prove how much, or what sort of profits could be expected on any one deal. Profits on trading would, of course, vary vastly, but Chris Dyer suggests that a 10 per cent profit on transactions might be the norm in the later middle ages, with possibly double that on wool sales.[27] Capital accumulation was based on the returns of trade, so that the bulk of a merchant's estate would be invested in goods rather than in land whilst he was active. When Roger Plente, merchant and four times mayor of Exeter died (c.1375) he was worth £1000, 60 per cent of which was in trading stock, another £80 in a ship and its freight, with a further £100 in cash.[28]

Trading profits could be supplemented by money earned from the provision of financial services, the provision of loans and exchange facilities. This was an area of business that had been controlled by moneyers, supplemented in the twelfth and for much of the thirteenth century by the Jewish community in England. With the ruin of the Jews on the one hand and the reorganisation and reduction in the number of mints on the other, the indigenous merchants became the most accessible and important source of loans at most levels. English crown borrowing too, though heavily dependent on alien bankers after the expulsion of the Jews, had by the later middle ages become largely, though not entirely, reliant on the English urban elite. Equally, Scottish merchants invested in loans to the Crown: Adam Forrester, an Edinburgh burgess who appeared to be a general factotum for the Crown, negotiating diplomatic, real estate and commercial deals, also lent substantial sums of money to the Scottish kings in the fourteenth century.[29] Usury laws notwithstanding, interest rates on loans were generally between 10 and 15 per cent by the fifteenth century in England, though there are records of up to 30–50 per cent being paid. As Nightingale points out, at these rates it was inevitable that merchants were encouraged to increase their investment in moneylending when times were difficult.[30]

Wealthy townsmen were also purchasers of property, but this does not mean that the accumulation of property was the most significant aspect of urban wealth. Certainly there were rentiers among the leaders of the urban community in the eleventh and twelfth centuries, but as we have seen, the composition and hence the financial base of that elite changed with the expansion of international trade. Urban property could serve many functions – a secure home, a signifier of financial respectability, a means of provision for dependants or a permanent bequest to a religious institution – but these things came as a result of money made in trade; the urban estate was built up after the fortune had been made, rather than being a significant plank in capital formation.

The freedom with which property and rights in property could be transferred in towns (a freedom somewhat circumscribed in Scotland by the reservation of the rights of heirs) meant that urban property portfolios were very fluid, and women's rights in property meant that they were an important element in the creation and dispersal of urban estates. These portfolios did not just comprise freeholds, but a variety of rents in tenements, parts of tenements, industrial premises and open spaces, with the rents coming from sub-lettings being a far more significant part of income than the original fossilised ground rent owing to the lord. There is evidence of the concentration of properties in the hands of richer burgesses in many places in the fourteenth and fifteenth centuries, for example in both Cork and Waterford the bulk of urban property came to be concentrated in the hands of a few individuals. The same trend has been observed in fourteenth- and fifteenth-century Scotland. However, even the most substantial urban portfolios were outweighed by the estates of institutions. It is probably significant in this context that one of the largest Waterford urban estates was bequeathed to St Saviour's chantry.[31] Property ownership could entail a great deal of expensive upkeep. Nor did returns always prove to be reliable; the rents owed did not necessarily correspond in any meaningful way with the actual sums collected, and indeed the shortfall apparent in fifteenth-century institutional rentals has been used as some of the most potent ammunition in the argument for serious decline in English towns. Medieval urban buildings were very flexible in the uses to which they could be put, and there seems to have been a similar flexibility in the way the urban estates of the elite were put together in a piecemeal way to capitalise on short-term opportunities and equally readily disbanded, in contrast to the consolidation that is evident in their accumulation of rural estates.

Images of urban society peddled by medieval churchmen and academics favoured a static hierarchy where each kept their place, dignified by their essential contribution to the body of the kingdom, though if, like artisans, they were the 'feet of the commonwealth', it was a thin sort of dignity. The same division of powerful and powerless was expressed in the terms *probi homines* and *minores*, commonly attached to the leaders of urban society and 'the rest'. Social mobility could involve two things, the rise of individuals through the acquisition of wealth to a higher status, or the growing status of entire social groups who could move into the category of *probi homines*. With regard to the former, although the pretensions of the *nouveaux riches* were publicly attacked, lowly birth was not a bar to success; society was theoretically open, but wealth was crucial. Rich individuals could be absorbed into the ranks of the better sort without causing a significant threat to the social order; a spectacular example, already encountered, was the de la Pole family. On a somewhat lesser scale, Richard Embleton of Newcastle probably started life as a villager and rose to be mayor of Newcastle in the thirteenth century on the strength of his fortune made in exporting wool and as a moneylender.[32] However, it is not enough to offer examples of such successes, like some medieval Samuel Smiles. What is more relevant is what sort of proportion of the lesser sort had any chance of climbing the social ladder – a calculation for which there is very little evidence for most of the period. By the later middle ages, where evidence is more forthcoming, as for example in Exeter and York, the prospects of moving into the civic elite from the common ruck were not promising, but it is a subject which could do with further investigation.

More significant in terms of changing social structure had been the emergence of the merchant class itself as a result of the growing commercialisation of the economy, a class which, by the thirteenth century, had largely replaced the crown servants, moneyers and knights who had formed the urban elite. It was a class which reinforced its financial base by intermarriage within and between towns. But increasing emphasis is being laid on the horizontal bonds that linked this urban elite with their counterparts in rural society from the thirteenth century onwards so that, by the fifteenth century, the concept of gentry could be applied as much to the better sort in towns, whether merchants or civil servants, as to the landed gentry. Arguably, by the fifteenth century there was 'no significant mental or cultural divide' between the urban and rural gentry in England; the same was true of Scotland, and to some extent the two cultures were beginning to create a gentry class in Wales by the sixteenth century.[33] Marriages of merchants into landed families or the purchase of estates should not be seen as a piece of social climbing by merchants but a recognition of shared aspirations and values: a sense of superior status, authority over the lesser sort, the holding of local public office, all rooted in the ownership of property. In Scotland the ubiquitous Adam Forrester held property across eastern Scotland, in part acquired from the ecclesiastics for whom he acted as financial agent, and he was knighted for his financial and diplomatic services to the Scottish Crown.

## Social Organisation

Given the discrepancy in wealth and opportunity and the fluid nature of the urban population, what prevented town life from constantly disintegrating into anarchy? Some pretty firm form of social cement was needed to act as a tie between individual households and to give some idea of the necessary sense of mutuality. Social pressure to conform was all the more imperative when the law operated as much as a fiscal device as a system of justice. Justice was too closely associated with the exercise of power to be the only, or the most effective, vehicle of social control; some consensus of values was needed, not only to contain the evil Nicholas Wodhills of the urban world, but also to structure the lives of the basically well-disposed. The Church was the prime supplier of social cement, its ideology translated into institutions that not only attempted to bind together living households, but extended these ties into eternity.

Currently there is much debate over the meaning of the term 'the urban community'. Did all townspeople acquiesce sufficiently in the consensus of values as taught by the Church to turn them into a coherent community? Scope for tension always existed. Although undoubtedly the message of the ecclesiastical authorities was of one of obedience, and of respect for a hierarchically ordered society, nevertheless the world-shunning renunciation at the heart of the Christian gospel had some potentially uncomfortable implications. We cannot be sure that the clergy's message was received with the same, or with a different understanding, to the way it was preached. Nor do we know whether everything that was heard was believed. So we are not in a strong position to make assumptions about the spirituality of the silent majority, or how much they questioned what they heard. Disaffection was only recorded when taken to radical lengths; more usually, a rejection of the Church's preached message would be registered by disassociation and go unrecorded.

But ultimately, whatever they thought about the Church on earth, few could afford to ignore what they had been taught about eternity. Family responsibilities did not end with death. From the twelfth century onwards the doctrine of purgatory, which had been 'creeping up on Western Christendom' since the early middle ages, came to be an increasingly important part of medieval spirituality.[34] Even for those eventually bound for heaven, satisfaction had to be made for sins committed on earth, and this was to be done in purgatorial fires. Lay demand for steps that could be taken to lessen what was anticipated as a deeply unpleasant experience led to great emphasis being placed on the good works that could count as advance payment, reducing the tariff of years to be spent in purgatory. The merit of these good works could also be applied for the succour of the souls of dead kin already languishing, and in theory was meant also to help all Christian souls departed. The continued dependence, once dead, on the intercessions of the living, not only of kin but also of neighbours, was the overriding consideration that moulded forms of worship by the fourteenth and fifteenth centuries.

The Church as the congregation of the faithful living and departed found its most characteristic expression in the parish. The number of parishes in any town in England was a matter of historical accident, having been frozen around 1200. This accounts for the contrast between Anglo-Saxon towns like Norwich, with 46 parishes, and the new town of Lynn, with one. The multiplicity of small churches in Anglo-Saxon towns were founded by powerful individuals and occasionally by groups of neighbours. Supervision over these churches passed into the hands of the ecclesiastical authorities during the course of the twelfth-century drive to reassert church control. They became parish churches, their territorial boundaries as fiercely defended by the incumbents as they had been by secular lords. Hence new parishes were seldom formed from 1200 onwards; newly founded market towns were part of a pre-existing parish that extended into the adjacent rural area. This could create the odd situation that a new town such as Hull might not have a parish church at all, being served by a chapel without rights of baptism and burial.[35]

Similar anomalies arose in Wales, where the parochial system was introduced along with other Anglo-Norman novelties like towns, but the two types of foundation did not always dovetail neatly. Aberystwyth had no parish church until the nineteenth century, and indeed probably no church at all before the mid-fifteenth, the townspeople having to trudge to Llanbardarn Fawr, the site of an important Celtic foundation some two miles away.[36] Equally, in Scotland the process of parish formation and the funding of parishes by a system of tithes was part of a package of new ideas introduced by David I into twelfth-century Scotland. This meant that most Scottish towns were part of a rural parish with, at times, an inconveniently located church: the residents of Coupar were not the only ones to rebuild their church inside the town in the course of the fifteenth century.[37]

The significance of the parish in the lives of townspeople has been substantially revised in recent years. Parishes are in the ascendant as genuinely expressive of a sense of communal identity and communal co-operation, the 'main point of reference for analysis of everyday devotional and social life'.[38] How did this operate in towns, where parishes varied so much in size and where the parish church might by the focus for a mix of townspeople and peasants? It is not possible to do more than speculate for the twelfth and thirteenth centuries. It may be that in the twelfth century the laity did not give much heed to the Church except in times of danger. It would be unwise to assume that in subsequent centuries we can see the emergence of a universal age of faith. There were always going to be lukewarm Christians, like those workmen castigated by Archbishop Minot of Dublin, who took holy days as holidays and 'many of whom never or rarely enter their parish church at hours when masses are celebrated, but spend almost all the feast day or at least the greater part thereof in taverns and drunkenness and other illicit acts of pleasure'.[39] However, all the evidence points to an increasing awareness among the laity of the fundamentals of Christianity and the involvement of a substantial proportion of them in parochial life. It is probable that the parish clergy became increasingly qualified as a result of several drives to raise standards, but equally the standards of what the laity expected rose. Their complaints, like those made in 1406 by the burgesses of Saltash, who pulled no punches in criticising their deaf, drunk and gossiping vicar, are testimony more to a well-informed spirituality than to a deep-rooted anticlericalism by the later middle ages.[40]

But the survival of English churchwardens' accounts from the fourteenth century show parishes involving the human and financial resources of their parishioners on a formidable scale. It is unfortunate that we have to quantify spiritual input largely in financial terms, but these accounts do provide a some measure of the extent to which the parish impinged on the parishioners, both voluntarily and involuntarily. Kumin has shown that the per capita sums raised by parishes were usually substantially higher than those raised by national taxation, and that these sums were particularly high in city-centre parishes. Urban money-raising came to differ in emphasis to that in the country, with the majority of income derived from the dead, that is, bequests of land and rents to sustain post-mortem commemoration. Compared to this, in rural areas income was primarily derived from the living, through fund-raising junketings such as church ales and plays. The urban churchwardens, with a portfolio of tenements to administer, together with levies and other sources of casual income had, by the fifteenth century, often considerably more money under their control than was due to the rector, and indeed subsidised the parochial clergy to obtain a better quality of service by enhancing the income of the serving priest or by buying in extra help.

By the later middle ages much of this money was also being poured into the beautification and sometimes wholesale rebuilding of the parish church, what Duffy has called 'an unprecedented lay investment' in the fabric.[41] This investment was as evident in Scotland as in England: to take one example, the parishioners of the Holy Rude in Stirling rebuilt their church after a fire.[42] The rather negative view which has prevailed as to the state of the Scottish parish in the fifteenth century needs to be balanced by this evidence of lay commitment to the Church. Rosser sees a similar commitment extending throughout English society: he argues that virtually every parishioner of Westminster contributed to the £200 it cost to rebuild St Margaret's between 1485 and 1525.[43] Decisions about rebuilding were made communally: the widow Alice Chester, a major benefactor of the parish of All Saints, Bristol, consulted 'the worshipful of this parish with other having best understanding and sights in carving' when it came to the design of the new rood loft that she paid for in 1483.[44]

However, Alice did only consult the most worshipful. In other respects the parish also reinforced existing hierarchies. Women were almost never involved as churchwardens. And although all male parishioners were expected to participate in parochial organisation, only the respectable held office. Certainly the increasing complexity of the real estate of urban parishes almost inevitably restricted the number of those who were likely to be entrusted with such office. In a small town like Sandwich, churchwardens were the same men who achieved the highest civic office; in larger towns parochial offices were the preserve of males of the middling rank, the weightiest parishioners tending to be preoccupied with civic posts rather than those at parochial level, a division of interests that served to accentuate the social division between the elite and the majority of burgesses.[45]

The sheer scale of the wealth of the richest townsmen meant that within the larger urban parishes there was a greater gulf between rich and poor than there was likely to be in rural parishes. It was a gulf underlined by the growing sense of hierarchy among those attending services. By the later middle ages private pews appeared, as for example at St Margaret's Southwark, where they were in place by the 1450s.[46] Recognition of obligation to the poor was there: in the church of All Saints, North Street, in York there is a window that vividly illustrates the corporal acts of mercy from St Matthew (25: 31–46), the hungry fed, the prisoners in the stocks being visited. Nor was this statement of human solidarity entirely window-dressing. Substantial sums of money were left in wills to distribute to the poor (though how effective this was will be discussed below), but this was seen as a personal obligation and not a parochial responsibility. And rather more money probably went into constructing the window than was dispensed in charity by the donor, and the good work glorifies the donor first and foremost.

In other ways, too, parish life focused attention on the wealthy and successful. The spiritual resources of the parish were supplemented by the chantry priests paid to sing masses for the souls of the wealthy dead, their kin and all faithful souls. Few of these priests were beneficed and perforce therefore were clustered in large towns where the concentration of potential patrons generated work. The chaplain set up in 1411 in All Saints, North Street, in York, by Adam del Bank, erstwhile mayor of York, was specifically instructed by the testator to co-operate with the other parish clergy, part of a team ministry. Not unexpectedly, the priest serving this chantry was to be presented not only by the rector but also by four senior parishioners. However, further than this he was to be formally appointed and could be removed by the mayor of York, as indeed was the case with the majority of the chaplains of chantries in the parish churches and chapels of York by the fifteenth century.[47] The civic authorities were increasingly moving in to control parish life, both details of fabric and services. In 1387 five new chapels built in St Giles, Edinburgh, were constructed under the auspices of the provost and council of the city who specified that they wanted vaults like those of St Stephen's, Holyrood. Aberdeen council in 1508 were concerned to maintain the quality of services and reserved all perpetual chantries to 'sangstairs that can sing planesang ande pricke sange at the lest'.[48]

The close interest taken by the civic elite in aspects of parochial worship is one reason for expressing a few reservations as to the extent to which the urban parish was always an effective vehicle for grass-roots involvement. The heavy dependence on surviving English churchwardens' accounts also means that conclusions drawn do not necessarily translate well to other parts of the British Isles. It is not possible to say how racial discrimination divided the parishes of the Welsh and Irish towns. Nor for Scotland is it possible to tell how inhibited the parochial community was by the fact that in most of the Scottish episcopal sees the parish church was part of the cathedral. In Glasgow there were six separate chapels dependent on the parish church founded by burgesses; such foundations might be seen as gestures towards a degree of lay autonomy by a laity determined to have their own spiritual arena, but again, we do not know how the community of these chapels was constituted in reality.[49]

Communities are constructed, they are not automatic, and they are defined by those they exclude as well as those they include. Within the parish itself there was the possibility for sub-groups to find their own often short-lived forms of self-expression, responding to particular needs. The most popular way of articulating the mutual support of such sub-groups was in the foundation of a fraternity or guild, the two terms being largely interchangeable, with the word 'fraternity' emphasising the communal aspects of the association. The ubiquity of these associations has been commented on earlier, and also the fact that they could be adapted to serve a variety of different functions according to the needs of the membership. The economic aspects of mercantile and craft guilds was concentrated on in Chapter 2, their administrative function in Chapter 3. But the primary function of guilds was to create social and religious bonds to weld together elements of the urban community. The parochial guilds that proliferated in medieval towns were not in opposition to the community of the parish; the majority of small religious fraternities were founded within parishes to supplement and support parochial services. Many of the smallest fraternities involved no more than a handful of people dedicated to the maintenance of a light within the parish church. The guild might be the best way to express a sense of solidarity specifically among townspeople in those market towns where the parish included the rural hinterland as well, so for example in Ashburton the guild of St Lawrence expressed the specific identity of the town.[50] Possibly elsewhere this sort of use of guilds would reinforce the linguistic divide between an English-speaking town and a countryside where the language was Welsh or Gaelic.

There were other non-parochial guilds and fraternities in towns, and people joined these in order to express their membership of the particular communities with which they wished to be identified. In larger towns individual crafts were numerous enough to sustain their own fraternities. Other urban guilds operated on wider criteria, some taking in members from all over the country; signing up royalty and aristocracy, as did the York Corpus Christi guild, would increase the guild's appeal and further extend membership. In contrast, there were guilds that were exclusive to particular social groups: the Trinity Guild of Coventry cost £5 to join and was restricted to the elder statesmen of the city.[51]

All guilds provided conviviality and support in this world, succour for the next. The amount of money and effort spent on these aspirations depended on the composition of the guild. The Ashburton guild effectively took the place of governmental institutions, providing not only a chaplain but a school, a market and the town's water supply. But even in towns where civic officers and council had long since adopted these functions, a close link remained between the members of prestigious guilds and the civic government, the social gatherings of the guild reinforcing the solidarity of the civic elite, and the holding of guild office a key step in the 'cursus honorum', or path of honour to the highest civic office. Whereas the top brass in Coventry belonged to the Trinity Guild, aspirants to high office who had not yet, and indeed might never, make the grade, belonged to the Corpus Christi guild.

The status of the guild would be made explicit in the kind of feasting that it could provide for its members – the importance of eating together to articulate a sense of community cannot be overemphasised. Rather more was spent on this aspect of fraternal life than on alms for poorer members. Nevertheless, there was a recognition of charitable obligations, spelled out clearly by the York carpenters' fraternity, who promised help at the rate of 4d a week to members who were unable to work because of the 'misfortunes of this world', though whether guild funds could sustain this kind of support to many hapless carpenters for any length of time must be doubtful.[52] Support also meant arbitration between guild members in order to keep conflict at a minimum and out of the town's courts. Equally, and importantly, it meant guarantors for those immigrants in difficulties and without families to speak for them. Finally, all guilds funded a decent battery of funeral services for the souls of deceased members and, where possible, the endowment of a priest to sing perpetually for those souls. Because of the cost, endowed guild chaplains tended to be urban, supported by either a large or a rich membership. Where cash was at a premium payment for this priest might be made in kind: the chaplains of some Scottish guild chapels were fed by a rota of neighbours.[53]

Nowadays the most widely known manifestation of guild spirituality are the cycles of plays associated with Corpus Christi. In fact these mega-productions were far from typical of the small didactic single plays that guilds normally put on. The parish in a small town might be the chief generator of public entertainment through the fund-raising devices mentioned above, or by sustaining plays and entertainers. The church of St Mary Magdalene, Launceston, benefited from a 40-day indulgence (a grant of time off purgatory) for those who supported the 'minstrels of St Mary Magdalene', a company whose fame is perhaps commemorated in the angel choir carved on the exterior of the east front.[54] There was probably no significant difference in the purpose or nature of these productions between those performed in a village and those in towns. Where larger towns did differ was both in the variety of the entertainment offered and in their capacity to stage large-scale processions and rituals. Great or small, ritual, processions and drama had secular as well as spiritual significance, as indeed the responsibilities of the civic elite were spiritual as well as secular. Dublin's ceremonial was characteristic. Every year the new mayor went with his officers in procession to listen to a sermon in the church of St Saviour's on the civic duties and rights of magistrates.[55] The propaganda was reinforced at festivals throughout the year, though Corpus Christi came to be one of the most popular, with the widest possible spectrum of townspeople involved. Crafts-people were involved in the production of suitably relevant stories from the cycle: fishermen as the apostles in Dublin, shipwrights in Dublin and York presenting the story of Noah. Undoubtedly street drama was popular and enthusiastically received, though the enthusiasm may not have been quite the sort that the organisers intended. Audience participation was taken to such a pitch in the York play of Fergus that in the early fifteenth century the masons who put it on begged to have another topic, as they could not cope with the ribaldry it evoked. The mermaid who appeared in the Perth Hammermen's play is a reminder of the ease with which popular tradition and myth could be incorporated into a religious procession, without any sense of incongruity.[56]

So there is reason to be confident that these productions did have widespread support and may well have served to create a sense of shared civic identity. If the best part of the citizenry could be brought on to the streets on Corpus Christi Day or other major festival, a statement was being made about the town itself as the body of Christ and the governing body of the town as custodians of morality and religion. To this end, Dobson sees the York Corpus Christi cycle as a deliberate 'creation of the civic elite'.[57] But the plays and processions can also be seen in a harsher light, as deliberately engineered propaganda exercises that papered over social division very thinly, presenting a myth of social harmony that was exposed when violence broke out during the processions. The violence was often a result of rivalry between participating groups, but it may on occasion have carried a more potent message, the presentation of an alternative ideology, using carnival to represent the world turned upside down. This may have been the case in Norwich in 1443, where a procession led by one John Gladman, decked out as a king, degenerated into a riot; one interpretation of events is to see Gladman as using the occasion to champion the cause of the artisans against an increasingly exclusive mercantile elite.[58]

Because the collapse of a public festival into disorder gave out all the wrong signals about the exercise of authority, city councils went to great pains to ensure that these spectacles were well funded and professionally produced. In doing so they introduced a degree of coercion not wholly compatible with the view that the festivals were genuine expressions of civic harmony. As with most human enterprises, the mix of motivation was complex, but when we find even the semi-skilled and unskilled manual labour of York formally organised so that they could contribute their mite to the masons' pageant at Corpus Christi, it must prompt questions as to whether the poorer artisans shared the same priorities, financial and social, as the civic elite.

Parish and guild look on first sight like devices for integration within towns. But their very success and ubiquity show the town refocused into a series of smaller communities, each of which had a particular place in the urban hierarchy. The brawls over precedence that occurred during public processions demonstrated that people were acutely aware of this hierarchy and anxious to define their status against their nearest rivals. But there could be no mistaking that mercers had infinitely more status than carpenters, and drapers far more than weavers. Nor could there be any mistaking that guilds overwhelmingly catered for the respectable and excluded the very poor. There were guilds for the poor such as that in the parish of St Augustine, Norwich, but they were unusual. Membership of a parochial guild gave status which distinguished a person from the common ruck of parishioners. Membership of a prestigious guild was the doorway to an altogether superior social and spiritual milieu.

Provision for the social integration of marginals was less committed and more haphazard. Town authorities targeted particular groups for exclusion altogether. Vagrants and prostitutes were unacceptable; poor members of ethnic minorities were generally regarded with suspicion; in the north-east of England particular hostility was reserved for the Scots. Others, who drifted in and out of poverty, were less clearly identifiable, and less threatening. Institutional charity was predominantly urban, reflecting what seems to have been a greater need amongst the urban poor, removed from the informal charity of the country. But in towns charity still remained a largely private affair, aimed at the personal salvation of the benefactor. As a result institutional provision for the poor was very sketchy. Hospitals and almshouses were founded from the eleventh century onwards, those for lepers, of course, designed to keep the unfortunate inmates at more than arm's length, rather than giving them a place within the community. Suspicion of 'intolerable persons' closed the doors of some hospitals, such as that at Bridgewater, to even the poor and infirm, although other institutions were more generous in their outlook.[59] But hospitals were first and foremost religious institutions, existing to provide for the souls of the founders, and as such tended to go upmarket in their intake, selling places in order to guarantee their income. Where finances were weak, organisation became ramshackle, and by the fifteenth century in England and Scotland there was a tendency for hospitals to be taken over by the town authorities in order to preserve them at all. In Edinburgh the council extended provision in 1435 specifically because 'many of the poor and weak die on account of the severe cold in these parts and lack of hospitals there'.[60] More usually and explicitly, such a step was taken in order to properly police the inmates.

A policing element seems also to have developed in other forms of charitable giving. Widespread handouts to the 'naked poor' and not specifically to the deserving were the favoured form of post-mortem charity among the laity before the Black Death, and Harvey sees this preference as continuing into the later middle ages. But others have detected a change as a result of the labour shortage after the Black Death, a change which militated against those too unlucky, feckless or raffish to be stakeholders in medieval society and who were increasingly sidelined by an ideology which shunned the spiritually unworthy.[61] Margery Kempe took the injunction to love your neighbour as yourself in a very literal

and partial way: 'It was more almes to helpun him that thei knewyn wel
for wel dysposyd folke and her owyn neybowrys than other strawngerys
whech thei knew not.'[62] There seems in places to have been an increased
disposition to favour poor and pious women by the later middle ages. In
short, charity was well in place as a means of social reward and control; it
was possibly less effective in keeping the poor alive in times of crisis.

Two issues arise from the foregoing discussion. First, although social
organisation in the town was moulded by the ideology of the Church,
this does not mean that it was determined solely by the church authorities. Clergy and laity came to co-operate very closely in late medieval
towns, but this co-operation was largely at a parochial level, where the
laity had a very strong hand. Major institutions, cathedrals and monasteries were for the most part distanced from civic ceremonial and ritual.
In this partnership, the laity, and the civic elite in particular, exercised a
great deal of power. So by the later middle ages the laity were increasingly
taking up and adapting those aspects of church teaching that served
their own spiritual and social needs. Given the extent of lay input into
parochial organisation, it is not surprising that in England and Wales it
was the parish that emerged as the key element of local government during the sixteenth century.

Second, what has to be constantly borne in mind is that what has been
described so far are the institutional devices that were put in place to
hold the social fabric of the town together. But institutions do not necessarily reflect how the society actually worked. Networks existed outside
formal associations, and these give a different perspective on urban
social structure. Much of women's working lives were inherently social:
marketing, using public washing places, selling ale. The network of
friendships established has a shadowy existence in the wills of the richer
women of late medieval English towns, with their personalised bequests
of rings, rosaries and clothes. There is the odd glimpse of interdepend-
ence among the humble. Joan White of Dublin left in her will 'my three
legged pan and one trough with two trundles for the use of my neighbours'.[63] The social fabric of the poor is almost wholly lost, though we
can see it filtered through the satire of the author of the Chester Corpus
Christi plays. Mrs Noah refuses to go into the Ark, preferring to stay with
her gossips, her drinking companions, who she feels are being unjustly
condemned to drown. Though the author makes this an issue of Mrs
Noah's wantonness, the need for such companionship, particularly
among the poor, for whom no other support was forthcoming, made
informal networks vital and made the alehouse a necessary part of social

life. Ale selling was on the whole informal, much of it from doorways, with consumption in the open air, but from the thirteenth century on, the alehouse became an increasingly prominent focus of socialising. The record of episcopal visitations, with their repeated injunctions to priests to stop hanging around alehouses and taverns, underlines the popularity of places of unbuttoned ease for people from all walks of life.


## Education – Secular and Religious

Talent without money, or with only limited funds, could be rewarded through education. The Church was the provider of schooling and determined the curriculum, though it was not a schooling wholly for the Church, and the majority of educated boys were not headed for the priesthood. But the church monopoly meant that elementary education was available where there was a cleric or a religious prepared and able to teach, rural or urban. Many schools were held by parish clergy, though by the later middle ages they were giving way to schools run by chaplains serving chantries and guild chapels. Just what the child learnt depended on both the skill of the available teacher and his or her objectives. Some elementary schools were established to give a training in song, choirs having become customary in even parochial churches by the fifteenth century, though as literacy was not essential for this skill, not all song schools taught reading. Where reading was taught it was in Latin till the late fourteenth century, at which time English was introduced into elementary schools in England. The use of vernacular Scots in the written record from the late fourteenth century suggests that this was likewise introduced at the same time.

Though by the fifteenth century the number of rural elementary schools was increasing rapidly, the sheer variety of ecclesiastical institutions in towns, and the numbers of unbeneficed clergy seeking to supplement their income, would presumably give the urban child a better chance of an education than their rural counterpart, as would the multiplication of post-mortem services that subsidised the parochial choirs and sustained the demand for song schools. And to obtain anything beyond elementary education meant travelling to town. Grammar schools were urban, initially attached to large ecclesiastical institutions, cathedrals, monasteries or collegiate churches. Before the fourteenth century it had generally been the case that these schools would provide all levels of education, elementary as well as advanced, with children learning their ABC at one extreme and advanced Latin constructions at the other. By the later middle ages grammar schools were shedding their elementary functions, taking only children who had reached a certain level of Latin literacy. These schools, too, were open to any child in theory; in practice town children were bound to be favoured because rural children had to meet the expense of boarding where scholarships were not available.

The popularity of grammar schools increased sharply in the course of the fifteenth century, with a positive explosion in provision after 1500. This enthusiasm is reflected in the respectable status accorded to schoolmasters by the late fifteenth century and a college to train grammar-school masters, Godshouse (subsequently Christ's College), was established in Cambridge in 1448.[64] In Scotland it may be the case that by 1500 most grammar schools had an MA in post, though the small town of Dunfermline was unusually lucky to have the services of the poet Robert Henryson.[65] It was a status derived from growing lay interest in education; significantly, most of the new schools founded in England after 1500 were founded by the laity to be run by the laity, often under the control of borough authorities. Equally importantly, in England this enthusiasm for grammar school was extending up the social scale, creating another bond between urban and rural gentry. The grammar school at Macclesfield in Cheshire was founded by John Percyvall, knight and mayor of London, to teach 'Gentilmens Sonnes and other godemennes children of the Towne and contre thereabouts'.[66] In terms of the curriculum, the provincial English schoolmaster seems to have been academically conservative; towns were not fostering hotbeds of intellectual innovation in this respect. The arrival of print seems only to have reinforced the cultural dominance of London among English towns; provincial stationers generally bought books through London, or commissioned them from foreign printers. This makes all the more appealing the anonymous St Albans schoolmaster who left teaching to set up a printing press in the 1480s, even experimenting with colour printing. Sadly, his venture fizzled out, probably defeated by the competition of imports.[67]

More townspeople were literate than country dwellers, and far more men than women. Girls could be educated in elementary schools with boys and there were female teachers, but they were a tiny minority. Best guesses put literacy for men in English towns at about 25 per cent by 1500, possibly substantially higher in London; in Scotland the levels of literacy were probably lower, though increasing rapidly by the beginning of the sixteenth century. The extent of literacy depended on the degree to which it was found useful. Literacy, of course, opened up a career in the Church and, Hoccleve notwithstanding, offered a way out of wearisome toil to those excluded from the merchant class. Just how attractive education was in opening possibilities is suggested in a rough measure of the destinations of York artisans' sons. In the later middle ages more took up some form of clerical career than established themselves in large-scale merchandising.

Specifically urban was the increasing importance of literacy to effective business. In Scotland, apart from the magnates, urban merchants were the only significant group of literate laity until the late fifteenth century. And in fifteenth-century London literacy was coming to be found even at a basic level, for by this date apprentices were expected to be able to read and write in English. In England special commercial courses were being offered in Oxford by the thirteenth century, and most of the students at the Inns of Court in the fifteenth century were probably intending to use their knowledge for commercial and administrative purposes. Administration and law were of course the other fields which fuelled the demand for literacy, and here there is a significant contrast between England and Wales on the one hand and Scotland on the other. Harding has emphasised how fundamentally important to social change was the 'fostering of professional groups' by English towns from the thirteenth century onwards in response to the growing complexity of government.[68] In particular, the end of the thirteenth century saw the emergence of professional lawyers in London and in some of the larger provincial towns.[69] Although each town had its own variants in law, based in local custom, all professional lawyers were trained in the royal courts, initially at Westminster and subsequently, from the mid-fourteenth century onwards, at the Inns of Court. Arguably, then, the proliferation of lawyers in provincial towns served in the long run to feed the growing cultural domination of London.

To judge by the books they possessed, some medieval townspeople also wanted to read in order to enhance their spiritual lives. As we have seen, one of the most striking aspects of medieval spirituality was the growing demand by laymen for control over access to salvation. Did towns provide a different or more heightened environment in which this demand could be pursued? The account given above of the social organisation of the town shows the scope for religious involvement, but were townspeople hearing a different message or experiencing religion in a different way to their rural counterparts? Did urban clergy pack a better punch?

The quality of the parochial clergy depended all too often on their incomes. If a parish was small or poor, as it often was when there were many parishes within one town, then it would not attract a high-flying rector. Many parishes were appropriated, which meant that they were served by a vicar on an annual and usually modest income. And although medieval Catholicism took preaching seriously, the priorities for the parochial and non-stipendiary clergy were to deliver the sacraments and to lead a decent life. Towns could offer alternative spiritual mentors, the most ubiquitous being the friars. Friars, being mendicant, were urban fauna; they shunned the landed endowment of earlier religious orders and in theory relied wholly on day-to-day charity. Financially independent, monasteries had been able to remain distanced from the towns that they might physically dominate and often legally control; in contrast, friars were part of an urban outreach, their message directed at the mass audience that could afford them the financial support they needed. Only in Ireland was this not the case; there friaries were largely rural, perhaps one of the most telling indicators of the divergence of the place of towns in Irish culture from the role they played in England, Wales and south and east Scotland.

It has been argued that the message that the friars preached was tailored from the outset to justify the profits of capitalism, a message to assuage the guilt of the urban rich. Friars' sermons were not in fact so narrowly focused as this interpretation implies, but the taking of theological debate, argued by highly trained preachers, literally into the market place could empower the urban laity in more indirect ways. It was presumably with the approval of York's civic elite that the Franciscan Thomas Richmond delivered a sermon in the municipal chapel that argued that the sacrament given by an impure priest was not a true sacrament.[70] The intention was not overtly heretical, though the sermon landed the friar before the church courts, and the whole episode is more evident of a lay desire to take control of their access to salvation than a rejection of fundamentals of Catholic dogma.

Did the higher literacy of townspeople and the access to more, more varied and provocative forms of preaching mean that towns became the foci of religious dissent? The equation cannot be made quite so neatly. The best documented medieval heresy in Britain is that of the English Lollard movement, which was not a purely urban phenomenon. Lollardy was a pretty ill-defined, diffuse movement but one that laid emphasis on access to scripture in the vernacular. The literate, nearly always men, led Lollard conventicles, but the illiterate shared the same text through being read to and by memorising, so that a charismatic figurehead was a more crucial condition of the spread of this heresy than a broad literate base. It should also be noticed that access to a vernacular Bible did not necessarily imply rejection of orthodoxy; Nicholas Blackburn junior, one of the family who filled All Saints, North Street, York with conventional expressions of piety was bequeathed an English version of the scriptures by his uncle, another member of the civic elite. These were the same people as had listened to Thomas Richmond; they felt entitled to criticise the Church, but their stake in the ritual life of the city was too great for them to seek to dismantle it, their power in the parish already being large enough to ensure that the Church served their spiritual needs.

In contrast, Lollardy attracted mainly male artisans; it did not, with the notable exception of the Lollard community in Leicester, attract more than a minority of women. McSheffrey argues that this was because, being mainly illiterate, women were denied power over the word.[71] Women seem rather to have found most spiritual scope in precisely those aspects of medieval Catholicism that text-based reformers rejected: the rich tradition of ritual life associated with the saints. The autobiography of Margery Kempe of Lynn demonstrates the point: she had spiritual classics read to her; the personal vision she developed from these stretched orthodoxy pretty far, but it was a vision rooted in the affective imaginative piety that was the chief characteristic of the late medieval Catholic Church.

At present the evidence seems to point to religious experience in the medieval town as being quantitatively rather than qualitatively different to that in the country. In order to persuade the key personnel of urban government to initiate the revolutionary policies of Protestantism in the sixteenth century a more potent mix of factors was needed. An escalation in access to new ideas through print, through growing literacy, and through the arrival of Protestant refugees was instrumental. The impact of new ideas becomes evident from the 1520s onwards, most significantly in towns, where higher concentrations of literacy meant a greater receptivity to printed propaganda. London was the most important hotbed of dissent, the concentration of imported ideas paralleling the concentration of trade in the capital. But for new religious practices to become widespread, equally important were signals from the court that challenges to ecclesiastical authority would be sanctioned by secular authority. So, in religion as in other spheres of life, it could be argued that provincial towns were following rather than leading cultural change by the end of the period. A similar scenario can be tentatively sketched for Scotland. There was a parallel development of assertiveness among a laity critical of inadequate pastoral care. But the desire for reform seems to have been largely contained within a Catholic theology. The change in direction to a specifically Protestant reformation came in the 1560s, spearheaded from the court by Protestant aristocrats.

The sheer physical appearance of the medieval town suggests that the experience of urban life in the middle ages should have been different to that in the country. The proximity and in many cases the congestion in which people lived made those lives very public. The larger the town, the more varied and cosmopolitan were possible encounters; the greater social mix meant greater extremes of wealth and poverty. Towns were certainly very conscious of their difference. Vast sums of money might be poured into the construction of visible boundaries, defences which were often statements of identity as much as a military necessity, a point most obviously made in Scotland, when there were often town gates but no walls. Civic ceremonial and urban panegyric articulated both difference and urban dignity.

But whereas walls signalled a distinction between town and country, the most prominent buildings within the town and the rituals acted out in those buildings served to underline the value-system shared by town and country alike. The churches, and by the end of the middle ages the guildhalls, were the physical expression of a society organised on the basis of divinely given social orders and of a hierarchy of status. By assigning them to a particular social order, merchants as *meliores*, artisans as *minores*, townspeople could be accommodated into the theory of harmonious estates beloved of moralising literature. It was a theory that gave an ideological framework to the mutual economic and political interests that served to link the urban *meliores* with their rural counterparts. For the most part these were the rural gentry, but exceptionally rich merchants would be able to equate with the aristocracy. So in considering how different the town was from the country, and whether the town can be seen as culturally innovative, the dynamic of the urban social mix has to be set against the conservatism of the ideology that operated to contain that mix. The literate and professional amongst townsmen can perhaps be better seen as conduits of the values of court, aristocracy and gentry rather than as generators of a specifically urban culture.

# CONCLUSION

The twelfth and thirteenth centuries saw towns established as a permanent part of the landscape, literally put on the map, throughout the British Isles, and moreover established in so secure a way that their role was not fundamentally undermined by even the most extreme economic and political vicissitudes of the later middle ages. By 1500 some ancient towns might not have been doing as well as they would have liked, and their nostalgia for past glories echoes loudly in the surviving records. Other less noisy newcomers were doing exceptionally well in England, and in Scotland the run of new town foundations continued throughout the sixteenth century. Even in Ireland, where the circumstances in which towns were founded had changed most radically of all by the fifteenth century, they not only survived to serve the needs of the diminishingly effective English colonisers, but also proved to be adaptable to the different economic priorities of the Gaelic Irish and the Anglo-Irish.

What sustained the towns was the growing commercialisation of society. In putting emphasis on commercialisation, attention is switched away from the division between country and town and drawn towards the factors that connected them. The engine of economic growth cannot be located definitively in either town or country; they were both part of the system of exchange. Hence, when conjuring up a picture of the medieval town it can be misleading to focus exclusively, or even perhaps primarily, on major cities like Dublin, Edinburgh and London, or on regional centres such as Aberdeen, Coventry or Bristol. The interaction of town and country is manifested more clearly in the small towns that made up the crucial first level of the urban hierarchy. This is not to say that town and country were indistinguishable, that there was a blurring of rural and urban identity. Towns, even small ones, were distinct because of their occupational structure, but it was a distinction that was generated and sustained by the mutual dependence of the urban and rural economies, rather than the result of an inherent competition between the two.

The emphasis on exchange also diverts attention away from technological innovation as a factor in urbanisation. Technological change,

spearheaded by towns that acted as crucibles of innovation, was seen by
Sjoberg as the key determinant of economic and social change in the
West.[1] But it cannot have escaped the reader that the interpretation of
the role of the medieval town put forward in this book has made little
reference to technological developments. The difference in emphasis
owes much to a difference in the scale of the comparisons undertaken.
Sjoberg's authoritative work embraces the development of the pre-
industrial city globally, and over thousands of years; the canvas here is
a very great deal more modest. It remains the case that in the centuries
between 1100 and 1500 there were no definitive technological leaps
forward that explain the establishment and growth of towns in Britain.
There were advances and improvements in terms of agriculture and of
transport, leading to greater specialisation of production; food processing and manufacturing were assisted by the more efficient use of power
in wind and water mills. But change was gradual, neither exclusively
rural or urban, contributing to rather than being the generator of a commercialising society.

The interaction of town and country, rather than their opposition,
applies also in large measure to the political community. Obviously this
generalisation cannot apply to the early colonisation of Ireland and
Wales, where towns were planted by an alien invader and where they
might remain the foci of resentment for centuries. But in Ireland the
Gaelicisation of the country in the later middle ages led to the construction of mutually advantageous links between Irish and Anglo-Irish
lords, and the leaders of urban communities. Shared aspirations could
emerge in the most unlikely places. In England and Scotland towns were
conceived from their foundation as part of the structure of feudal society, expressions of feudal lordship. The nature of lordship, of social relations and of political power, changed profoundly over the 400 years
between 1100 and 1500; but towns can best be understood as adapting
or being adapted to new political and social formations, rather than as
hotbeds of radical ideas that threatened to undermine lordship altogether. Innovations in urban government served to reinforce exisiting
hierarchies. Urban elites shared the same aspirations as their rural
equivalents. They sought association with the knights and with gentry
(or, for the most potent among them, with the aristocracy); they too
served as agents in the royal judical and administrative machine. The
significance of lordship was as pressing an issue for towns in 1500 as it
had been in 1100. The dismembered bodies of traitors on gates – parts of
David of Wales distributed to the four quarters of England in 1283, the

Duke of York's head fixed to Bootham Bar in York in 1460 – made the
point crudely but graphically, a savage counterpoint to the elaborate rituals that towns had developed to trumpet their importance as part of the
community of the realm.

For towns might have a very elevated idea of their own significance,
and with some just cause. Larger towns in particular were conscious of
offering a concentration of facilities and opportunities, education and a
training ground for professionals not found elsewhere. It has been
argued in the course of this book that in large measure the values and
aspirations of townspeople did not differ in kind to the cultural norms of
their counterparts in rural society, and that this was most evident
amongst the urban elite. Despite these shared norms, the diversity not
only of occupation, but also of opportunity, meant that towns felt different to live in. The concentration of facilities, and the variety of lifestyles,
were sufficiently great to make urban culture qualitatively and not just
quantitatively different, and to excite what now seem to be somewhat
extravagant parallels with ancient cities. The writer of the Lanercost
Chronicle, who felt that Berwick, on account of its 'populous and busy'
nature, had merited the name of 'a second Alexandria', had, like Pecham,
a mindset framed by classical values.[2] Both could see the potential of
the urban environment – a potential, however, largely deployed for,
and harnessed by, the interests of the powerful.

This book has boldly generalised over four countries and 400 years,
though an attempt has been made to keep the variety of local experience
constantly in mind. It will conclude with yet one more large generalisation that tries to put a shape on the whole period. Whereas in 1200 the
similarities between towns founded across the British Isles are striking,
by 1500 political, economic and social change had given towns in the
four countries of the British Isles different identities. The decades between 1270 and 1350 proved to be crucial in this, both for political and
economic reasons, marking the divergence of the experience of Scottish
and Irish towns from that of English towns, and reasserting the place of
Welsh towns as expressions of the domination of English culture in
Wales. But for nearly all towns outside Ireland, the combination of economic and social factors that concentrated power and wealth in the capitals in the later middle ages meant that, although their sense of their own
worth was made increasingly explicit in the machinery and pomp of government, it was not matched by a growing cultural independence. By
the early sixteenth century, London and Edinburgh were overwhelmingly dominant in their respective kingdoms.

# NOTES AND REFERENCES

## Introduction

1. P. Bairoch, J. Batou and P. Chèvre, *The Population of European Cities from 800 to 1850* (Geneva, 1988), pp. 183–206.
2. R. H. Britnell, *The Commercialisation of English Society 1000–1500* (Cambridge, 1993).
3. R. H. Hilton, *English and French Towns in Feudal Society: A Comparative Study* (Cambridge, 1992).
4. R. H. Hilton, *Class Conflict and the Crisis of Feudalism* (London, 1985), p. 202.
5. G. W. S. Barrow, *Kingship and Unity: Scotland 1000–1306* (London, 1981), p. 85.
6. M. M. Postan, *The Medieval Economy and Society* (London, 1972), p. 212.
7. S. H. Rigby, *English Society in the Later Middle Ages* (Macmillan, 1995).

## 1  Urbanisation

1. H. Clarke and B. Ambrosiani, *Towns in the Viking Age* (Leicester, 1991), p. 15.
2. J. Blair, 'The minsters of the Thames', in J. Blair and B. Golding (eds), *The Cloister and the World* (Oxford, 1996), pp. 12–14.
3. Clarke and Ambrosiani, *Towns in the Viking Age*, pp. 42, 100–1.
4. C. Dyer, 'Recent developments in early medieval urban history and archaeology in England', in D. Denecke and D. Shaw (eds), *Urban Historical Geography: Recent Progress in Britain and Germany* (Cambridge, 1988), pp. 74–5.
5. B. J. Graham, 'The town and the monastery: early medieval urbanisation in Ireland, AD 800–1150', in T. E. Slater and G. Rosser (eds), *The Church in the Medieval Town* (Aldershot, 1998), pp. 131–4.
6. H. B. Clarke, 'Decolonisation and the dynamics of urban decline in Ireland, 1300–1550', in T. E. Slater (ed.), *Urban Decline 100–1600* (forthcoming).
7. E. Miller and J. Hatcher, *Medieval England: Towns, Commerce and Crafts 1086–1348* (London, 1995), pp. 393–4.
8. R. Britnell, 'The proliferation of markets in England, 1200–1349', *Economic History Review*, 2nd ser., 34 (1981), p. 210; Miller and Hatcher, *Medieval England: Towns, Commerce and Crafts*, p. 159.
9. For the theory of urban hierarchies, see Chapter 2.
10. N. J. Mayhew, 'Modelling monetization', in R. H. Britnell and B. M. S. Campbell (eds), *A Commercialising Economy: England 1086–c.1300* (Manchester, 1995), pp. 70–1; Britnell, *Commercialisation*, pp. 102–3.

11. R. M. Spearman, 'The medieval townscape of Perth', in M. Lynch, M. Spearman and G. Stell, *The Scottish Medieval Town* (Edinburgh, 1988), pp. 42–59.

12. G. Duby, *The Early Growth of the European Economy* (London, 1974).

13. K. J. Stringer, *David, Earl of Huntingdon* (Edinburgh, 1985), p. 70.

14. R. R. Davies, *Conquest, Coexistence and Change: Wales 1066–1415* (Oxford, 1987), p. 168.

15. M. Altschul, *A Baronial Family in Medieval England: The Clares 1217–1314* (Baltimore, 1965), p. 285.

16. J. Bradley, 'Planned Anglo-Norman towns in Ireland', in H. B. Clarke and A. Simms (eds), *The Comparative History of Urban Origins in Non-Roman Europe*, BAR International Series 255 (1985), pp. 420–1; Clarke, 'Decolonisation and the dynamics of urban decline'.

17. I. Soulsby, *The Towns of Medieval Wales* (Winchester, 1983), p. 18.

18. H. Summerson, 'The place of medieval Carlisle in the commerce of northern England in the thirteenth century', in P. R. Coss and S. D. Lloyd (eds), *Thirteenth Century England I* (Woodbridge, 1986), p. 142.

19. D. H. Owen, 'The middle ages', in D. H. Owen (ed.), *Settlement and Society in Wales* (Cardiff, 1989), p. 217.

20. Miller and Hatcher, *Medieval England: Towns, Commerce and Crafts*, p. 273.

21. E. Rutledge, 'Immigration and population growth in early fourteenth century Norwich: evidence from a tithing roll', *Urban History Yearbook* (1988), p. 27.

22. P. Nightingale, 'The growth of London in the medieval English economy', in R. Britnell and J. Hatcher (eds), *Progress and Problems in Medieval England: Essays in Honour of Edward Miller* (Cambridge, 1996), pp. 95–8.

23. Soulsby, *Towns of Medieval Wales*, pp. 22–3; Davies, *Conquest, Coexistence and Change*, p. 167.

24. P. G. B McNeill and H.L. MacQueen (eds), *Atlas of Scottish History to 1707* (Edinburgh, 1996), pp. 196–8; E. Gemmill and N. Mayhew, *Changing Values in Medieval Scotland: a Study of Prices, Money, Weights and Measures* (Cambridge, 1995), p. 9.

25. R. E. Glasscock, 'Land and people c.1300', in A. Cosgrove (ed.), *A New History of Ireland. II. Medieval Ireland 1169–1534* (Oxford, 1993), p. 235.

26. McNeill and MacQueen (eds), *Atlas of Scottish History*, pp. 198, 213, 214.

27. M. Bailey, 'Peasant welfare in England, 1290–1348', *Economic History Review*, 2nd ser., 51 (1998), p. 236.

28. Britnell, *Commercialisation*, pp. 166–7.

29. A. Dyer, *Decline and Growth in English Towns, 1400–1640* (Cambridge, 1991) sums up the debate.

30. J. Hatcher, 'The great slump of the mid fifteenth century', in Britnell and Hatcher (eds), *Progress and Problems*, p. 267; C. Phythian-Adams, *Desolation of a City: Coventry and the Urban Crisis of the Later Middle Ages* (Cambridge, 1979).

31. M. Bailey, 'A tale of two towns: Buntingford and Standon in the later middle ages', *Journal of Medieval History*, 19 (1993), pp. 351–71.

32. C. Dyer, 'Small towns 1270–1540', in *Cambridge Urban History* (forthcoming).

33. Dyer, *Decline and Growth*, pp. 29–34.

34. Davies, *Conquest, Coexistence and Change*, p. 372.

35. R. R. Davies, *The Revolt of Owain Glyn Dŵr* (Oxford, 1995), pp. 282–3.

36. Soulsby, *Towns of Medieval Wales*, pp. 25–6.
37. Clarke, 'Decolonisation and the dynamics of urban decline'.

## 2 The Urban Economy

1. E. P. Dennison and R. Colman, *Historic Dunblane*, Scottish Burgh Survey (Edinburgh, 1998).
2. Miller and Hatcher, *Medieval England: Towns, Commerce and Crafts*, p. 176.
3. C. Dyer, 'Medieval Stratford: a successful small town', in R. Bearman (ed.), *The History of an English Borough, Stratford upon Avon 1196–1996* (Stroud, 1997), p. 56.
4. S. Kelly (ed.), *Men of Property: An Analysis of the Norwich Enrolled Deeds 1285–1311* (n.d.), pp. 34–5.
5. E. M. Veale, 'Craftsmen and the economy of London in the fourteenth century', in R. Holt and G. Rosser (eds), *The Medieval Town 1200–1540* (London, 1990), pp. 131, 135.
6. J. Masschaele, *Peasants, Merchants and Markets: Inland Trade in Medieval England 1150–1350* (New York, 1997), pp. 4–6.
7. C. Dyer, 'Market towns and the countryside in late medieval England', *Canadian Journal of History*, 31 (1996), pp. 18–35.
8. A Tuck, 'A medieval tax haven; Berwick upon Tweed and the English crown 1333–1461', in Britnell and Hatcher (eds), *Progress and Problems*, pp. 154–61.
9. D. Roffe, *Stamford in the Thirteenth Century* (Stamford, 1994), pp. 51, 65.
10. M. Kowaleski, *Local Markets and Regional Trade in Medieval Exeter* (Cambridge, 1995), p. 181.
11. Davies, *Conquest, Coexistence and Change*, p. 373.
12. E. P. Dennison and R. Colman, *Historic Coupar Angus*, Scottish Burgh Survey (Edinburgh, 1998).
13. D. G. Shaw, *The Creation of a Community: The City of Wells in the Middle Ages* (Oxford, 1993), p. 91.
14. M. Lynch, 'The social and economic structure of the larger towns', in Lynch, Spearman and Stell, *Scottish Medieval Town*, p. 275.
15. Tuck, 'A medieval tax haven', p. 150.
16. Masschaele, *Peasants, Merchants and Markets*, pp. 150–8.
17. Gemmill and Mayhew, *Changing Values*, p. 67.
18. R. Holt, 'Gloucester in the century after the Black Death', in Holt and Rosser (eds), *The Medieval Town 1200–1540*, p. 145.
19. Gemmill and Mayhew, *Changing Values*, pp. 40, 71.
20. R. H. Hilton, *Class Conflict and the Crisis of Feudalism* (London, 1985), pp. 194–215.
21. *Statutes of the Realm I*, 37 Ed. III c.6, p. 379.
22. G. Rosser, *Medieval Westminster 1200–1540* (Oxford, 1989), p. 202 ; R. I. Jack, 'The cloth industry in medieval Wales', *Welsh Historical Review*, 10 (1980–1), p. 455; H. C. Swanson, *Medieval Artisans: an Urban Class in Late Medieval England* (Oxford, 1989), p. 103.
23. Rosser, *Medieval Westminster*, p. 142.
24. Lynch, 'The social and economic structure of the larger towns', p. 277.

25. Swanson, *Medieval Artisans*, p. 22; J. M. Bennett, 'Women and men in the Brewers' gild of London c.1420', in E. B. DeWindt (ed.), *The Salt of Common Life* (Kalamazoo, 1995), p. 190.
26. Swanson, *Medieval Artisans*, p. 24; Britnell, *Commercialisation*, p. 163; Kowaleski, *Local Markets and Regional Trade*, p. 146.
27. C. Dyer, 'Market towns and the countryside in late medieval England', *Canadian Journal of History*, 31 (1996), p. 25.
28. D. Postles, 'An English small town in the later middle ages: Loughborough', *Urban History*, 20 (1993), pp. 7–29.
29. Dyer, 'Medieval Stratford', p. 55.
30. C. Dyer, *Everyday Life in Medieval England* (London, 1994), p. 260.
31. R. H. Britnell, *Growth and Decline in Colchester, 1300–1525* (Cambridge, 1986), p. 39.
32. Borthwick Institute, York, Dean and Chapter Register of Condemnations, f.6; Jack, 'Cloth industry in medieval Wales', p. 454; Swanson, *Medieval Artisans*, p. 136.
33. Kowaleski, *Local Markets and Regional Trade*, p. 300.
34. E. Ewan, *Townlife in Fourteenth Century Scotland* (Edinburgh, 1990), p. 123.
35. E. King, 'Economic development in the early twelfth century', in Britnell and Hatcher (eds), *Progress and Problems*, p. 14; T. O'Neill, *Merchants and Mariners in Medieval Ireland* (Dublin, 1986), pp. 63–4.
36. Britnell, *Commercialisation*, p. 83; Masschaele, *Peasants, Merchants and Markets*, pp. 207–10.
37. J. L. Bolton, *The Medieval English Economy, 1150–1500* (London, 1980), p. 319.
38. Miller and Hatcher, *Medieval England: Towns, Commerce and Crafts*, pp. 18, 197.
39. Bolton, *Medieval English Economy*, p. 289.
40. Kowaleski, *Local Markets and Regional Trade*, ch. 6.
41. C. Platt, *Medieval Southampton* (London, 1973), pp. 160–2.
42. Gemmill and Mayhew, *Changing Values*, pp. 73–4; A Murray, 'The customs accounts of Kirkudbright, Wigtown and Dumfries 1434–1560', *Transactions of the Dumfries and Galloway Natural History and Antiquarian Society*, 3rd ser., 40 (1961–2), p. 155.
43. A. Stevenson, 'Trade with the south, 1070–1513', in Lynch, Spearman and Stell, *Scottish Medieval Town*, p. 196.
44. A. R. Saul, 'English towns in the later middle ages: the case of Great Yarmouth', *Journal of Medieval History*, 8 (1982), pp. 83–6.
45. O'Neill, *Merchants and Mariners*, pp. 53–4.
46. E. M. Carus-Wilson and O. Coleman, *England's Export Trade 1275–1547* (Oxford, 1963), pp. 75, 138–41.
47. McNeill and MacQueen (eds), *Atlas of Scottish History*, pp. 238–60.
48. W. Childs and T. O'Neill, 'Overseas trade', in A. Cosgrove (ed.), *A New History of Ireland. II. Medieval Ireland 1169–1534* (Oxford, 1993), p. 494.
49. E. M. Carus-Wilson, *Medieval Merchant Venturers*, 2nd edn (London, 1967), p. 10.
50. Barrow, *Kingship and Unity*, p. 131; McNeill and MacQueen (eds), *Atlas of Scottish History*, pp. 239, 264.

51. Carus-Wilson, *Medieval Merchant Venturers*, p. 93.
52. G. A. Williams, *Medieval London: from Commune to Capital* (London, 1970), pp. 122–3.
53. Carus-Wilson, *Medieval Merchant Venturers*, pp. 80–1, 84–90.
54. Phythian-Adams, *Desolation of a City*, pp. 44, 119–21.
55. Dyer, 'Medieval Stratford', p. 58.
56. Childs and O'Neill, 'Overseas trade', pp. 492, 517–18.
57. Miller and Hatcher, *Medieval England: Towns, Commerce and Crafts*, p. 231.
58. T. H. Lloyd, *The English Wool Trade in the Middle Ages* (Cambridge, 1977), p. 170; Miller and Hatcher, *Medieval England: Town, Commerce and Crafts*, p. 247.
59. P. Nightingale, *A Medieval Mercantile Community: the Grocers' Company and the Politics and Trade of London 1000–1485* (London, 1995), p. 532.
60. P. Nightingale, 'The growth of London in the medieval English economy', in Britnell and Hatcher (eds), *Progress and Problems*, p. 103.
61. J. Raine (ed.), *Testamenta Eboracensia*, vol. III (Surtees Society, 45, 1860), pp. 101–5.
62. *Statutes of the Realm* I, p. 379, 37 Edward III c.6.
63. R. M. Spearman, 'Workshops, materials and debris', in Lynch, Spearman and Stell (eds), *Scottish Medieval Town*, p. 143; J. Schofield and A.Vince, *Medieval Towns* (Leicester, 1994), p. 123; P. Wallace, 'The archaeology of Anglo-Norman Dublin', in Clarke and Simms (eds), *Comparative History of Urban Origins*, pp. 394–6, 399.
64. Hilton, *Class Conflict*, p. 188; Miller and Hatcher, *Medieval England: Towns, Commerce and Crafts*, p. 259.
65. Dyer, *Everyday Life*, p. 264.
66. Britnell, *Growth and Decline in Colchester*, pp. 55–7.
67. R. A. Brown, H. M. Colvin and A. J. Taylor (eds), *The History of the King's Works. Vol. I. The Middle Ages* (London, 1963), pp. 411, 414.
68. Swanson, *Medieval Artisans*, pp. 71, 74.
69. *Ibid.*, p. 72.
70. F. Bickley (ed.), *The Little Red Book of Bristol*, vol. II (Bristol, 1900), p. 127.
71. M. K. Dale, 'The London silkwomen of the fifteenth century', *Economic History Review*, 4 (1933), pp. 324–35.
72. M. Bonney, *Lordship and the Urban Community: Durham and its Overlords 1250–1540* (Cambridge, 1990), p. 165.
73. Borthwick Institute, York, Dean and Chapter Original wills and inventories.
74. Veale, 'Craftsmen and the economy of London', pp. 133–4.
75. Ewan, *Townlife in Fourteenth Century Scotland*, p. 124.
76. Swanson, *Medieval Artisans*, p. 52.
77. M. Sellers (ed.), *York Memorandum Book*, vol. I (Surtees Society, 120, 1911), pp. 193–4.
78. J. Lydon, *Ireland in the Later Middle Ages* (Dublin, 1971), p. 18.
79. Britnell, *Growth and Decline in Colchester*, p. 102.
80. J. H. Munro, *Textiles, Towns and Trade* (Aldershot, 1994), p. 242.
81. See below, Chapter 3.
82. Jack, 'Cloth industry in medieval Wales', p. 456.
83. Britnell, *Growth and Decline in Colchester*, p. 78.

84. Jack, 'Cloth industry in medieval Wales', p. 451.
85. M. Zell, 'Credit in the pre-industrial English woollen industry', *Economic History Review*, 2nd ser., 49 (1996), pp. 673–4.
86. R. H. Hilton, 'Low level urbanisation: the seigneurial borough of Thornbury in the middle ages', in Z. Razi and R. Smith, *Medieval Society and the Manor Court* (Oxford, 1966), pp. 501–2.
87. R. M. Karras, *Common Women: Prostitution and Sexuality in Medieval England* (Oxford, 1996), pp. 66–7; L. Attreed, *The York House Books 1461–90* (Sutton, 1991), p. 708.
88. F. Collins (ed.), *Register of the Freemen of the City of York*, vol. I (Surtees Society, 96, 1896), pp. 194, 229.
89. N. P. Tanner, *The Church in Late Medieval Norwich* (Toronto, 1984), pp. 20–1.
90. A. K. McHardy, 'Ecclesiastics and economics', in W. J. Sheils and D. Wood (eds), *The Church and Wealth* (Oxford, 1987), p. 131.
91. Quoted in Rosser, *Medieval Westminster*, p. 206.
92. A. Harding, *England in the Thirteenth Century* (Cambridge, 1993), p. 149.
93. R. A. Griffiths (ed.), *Boroughs of Mediaeval Wales* (Cardiff, 1978), pp. 78–9, 155–7.
94. R. C. Stacey, 'Jewish lending and the medieval English economy', in Britnell and Campbell (eds), *Commercialising Economy*, pp. 78–101.
95. E. B. Fryde, *William de la Pole: Merchant and King's Banker* (London, 1988), p. 1.
96. Ewan, *Townlife in Fourteenth Century Scotland*, pp. 112, 121, 126–8.
97. Gemmill and Mayhew, *Changing Values*, pp. 374.
98. Britnell, *Growth and Decline in Colchester*, pp. 266–7.
99. Miller and Hatcher, *Medieval England: Towns, Commerce and Crafts*, p. 274.

## 3   Urban Government

1. J. Tait, *The Medieval English Borough* (Manchester, 1936); A. Ballard (ed.), *British Borough Charters 1042–1216* (Cambridge, 1913); A. Ballard and J. Tait (eds), *British Borough Charters 1216–1307* (Cambridge, 1923).
2. Griffiths (ed.), *Boroughs of Mediaeval Wales*, pp. 13, 250.
3. Hilton, *Class Conflict*, pp. 191–2.
4. *Ibid.*, p. 200.
5. Ballard (ed.), *British Borough Charters*, p. 102.
6. G. H. Martin, 'The English borough in the thirteenth century', in Holt and Rosser (eds), *Medieval Town*, pp. 34–5.
7. Ballard, *British Borough Charters*, p. 205.
8. C. Gross, *The Gild Merchant*, vol. I (Oxford, 1890), p. 31.
9. R. B. Dobson, 'Admissions to the freedom of the city of York in the later middle ages', *Economic History Review*, 2nd ser., 26 (1973), p. 20.
10. G. MacNiocaill, 'Socio-economic problems of the late medieval Irish town', in D. Harkness and M. O'Dowd (eds), *The Town in Ireland* (Belfast, 1981), pp. 16–20.
11. D. Greenway and J. Sayers (eds), *Joscelin of Brakelond, Chronicle of the Abbey of Bury St. Edmunds* (Oxford, 1989), pp. 89–90.
12. D. Keene, 'Suburban growth', in Holt and Rosser (eds), *Medieval Town*, p. 111.

13. Bonney, *Lordship and the Urban Community*, pp. 199–201, 243.
14. Rosser, *Medieval Westminster*, pp. 155–6.
15. Rosser, *Medieval Westminster*, pp. 234–44; M. Carlin, *Medieval Southwark*, (London, 1996), p. 108.
16. McNeill and MacQueen (eds), *Atlas of Scottish History*, p. 192; H. L. MacQueen and W. J. Windram, 'Laws and courts in the burghs', in Lynch, Spearman and Stell (eds), *Scottish Medieval Town*, pp. 213–15.
17. M. Bateson (ed.), *Records of the Borough of Leicester 1103–1327* (London, 1899), pp. xxvii–xl.
18. Britnell, *Growth and Decline in Colchester*, p. 26; Gemmill and Mayhew, *Changing Values*, p. 27.
19. S. Reynolds, *An Introduction to the History of English Medieval Towns* (Oxford, 1977), p. 104; Ballard, *British Borough Charters*, p. 220.
20. R. Dudley Edwards, 'The beginnings of municipal government in Dublin', in H. Clarke (ed.), *Medieval Dublin: the Living City* (Oxford, 1990), pp. 146–7.
21. Ewan, *Townlife in Fourteenth Century Scotland*, p. 42.
22. A. A. M. Duncan, *Scotland, the Making of the Kingdom* (Edinburgh, 1975), p. 496.
23. Reynolds, *English Medieval Towns*, p. 121. For coroners see below, p. 82.
24. Griffiths, *Boroughs of Mediaeval Wales*, pp. 69, 125.
25. Gemmill and Mayhew, *Changing Values*, p. 27.
26. E. P. D. Torrie, 'The guild in fifteenth century Dunfermline', in Lynch, Spearman and Stell (eds), *Scottish Medieval Town*, pp. 249, 253.
27. G. Harriss, 'Political society and the growth of government in late medieval England', *Past and Present*, 138 (1993), p. 56
28. V. Harding and L. Wright, *London Bridge: Selected Accounts and Rentals 1381–1528*, London Record Society, 1995, pp. 65–110 *passim*.
29. Gemmill and Mayhew, *Changing Values*, p. 43.
30. Reynolds, *English Medieval Towns*, pp. 104–5.
31. Williams, *Medieval London*, p. 3.
32. *Ibid.*, pp. 204–8.
33. Dyer, 'Medieval Stratford', pp. 54–5.
34. Rigby, *English Society*, pp. 167–9.
35. A. F. O'Brien, 'Royal boroughs, the seaport towns and royal revenue in medieval Ireland', *Journal of the Royal Society of Antiquaries of Ireland*, 118 (1988), pp. 24–5.
36. J. Wormold, *Lords and Men: Bonds of Manrent 1442–1603* (Edinburgh, 1985), pp. 137–43.
37. Quoted in A. Grant, 'To the medieval foundations', *Scottish Historical Review*, 73 (1994), p. 6.
38. Britnell, *Commercialisation*, p. 208.
39. Rigby, *English Society*, pp. 9–14.
40. C. J. Wickham, 'Gossip and resistance among the medieval peasantry', *Past and Present*, 160 (1998), pp. 3–24.
41. Hilton, *English and French Towns*, p. 56.
42. MacNiocaill, 'Socio-economic problems', p. 9.
43. R. H. Britnell, 'Sedentary long-distance trade and the English merchant class in thirteenth century England', in P. R. Coss and S. D. Lloyd (eds), *Thirteenth Century England V* (Woodbridge, 1995), p. 139.

44. R. F. Hunniset, *The Medieval Coroner* (Cambridge, 1961), p. 141.
45. J. A. Watt, 'Approaches to the history of fourteenth century Ireland', in Cosgrove (ed.) *New History of Ireland. II*, p. 308.
46. G. O. Sayles, 'The dissolution of a gild at York in 1306', *English Historical Review*, 4 (1940), pp. 83–92.
47. Williams, *Medieval London*, pp. 193–5, 282; Reynolds, *English Medieval Towns*, p. 137.
48. Reynolds, *English Medieval Towns*, pp. 133–5.
49. P. Nightingale, 'Capitalists, crafts and constitutional change in late fourteenth century London', *Past and Present*, 124 (1989), pp. 3–35. The quotation is from R. Bird, *The Turbulent London of Richard II* (London, 1949).
50. Quoted in Rigby, *English Society*, p. 170.
51. C. Barron, 'Ralph Holland and the London radicals 1438–1444', in Holt and Rosser (eds), *Medieval Town*, pp. 160–83.
52. Kowaleski, *Local Markets and Regional Trade*, p. 101.
53. Rigby, *English Society*, p. 175.
54. Britnell, *Growth and Decline in Colchester*, pp. 120–1.
55. W. Hudson and J. C. Tingay (eds), *The Records of the City of Norwich*, vol. I (Norwich, 1906), p. 81.
56. Rigby, *English Society*, p. 175.
57. Kowaleski, *Local Markets and Regional Trade*, p. 117.
58. McNiocaill, 'Socio-economic problems', p. 18.
59. Barrow, *Kingship and Unity*, p. 125.
60. G. Rosser, 'Crafts, guilds and the negotiation of work in the medieval town', *Past and Present*, 154 (1997), pp. 3–31.
61. *VCH Northamptonshire*, vol. III (London, 1930), p. 28.
62. Swanson, *Medieval Artisans*, p. 113.
63. Gemmill and Mayhew, *Changing Values*, p. 45.
64. Swanson, *Medieval Artisans*, p. 123.
65. M. Verschuur, 'Merchants and craftsmen in sixteenth century Perth', in M. Lynch (ed.), *The Early Modern Town in Scotland* (London, 1986), p. 43.
66. Hilton, *English and French Towns*, pp. 146–8.
67. Sellers (ed.), *York Memorandum Book*, vol. I, pp. 190–7.
68. Britnell, *Growth and Decline in Colchester*, p. 221.
69. S. Jones, 'Out of the footnotes. The women woolpackers of sixteenth century Southampton', *Gender and History* (forthcoming).
70. O'Brien, 'Royal boroughs, the seaport towns and royal revenue', p. 23.
71. Carlin, *Medieval Southwark*, pp. 116–19.

## 4 Urban Society

1. Royal Commission on the Ancient and Historical Monuments of Scotland, *Tollbooths and Town Houses: Civic Architecture in Scotland to 1833* (Edinburgh, 1996), pp. 2, 12, 82.
2. Schofield and Vince, *Medieval Towns*, p. 64; R. M. Spearman, 'The medieval townscape of Perth', in Lynch, Spearman and Stell (eds), *Scottish Medieval*

*Town*, p. 55; J. Bradley, 'Planned Anglo-Norman towns in Ireland', in Clarke and Simms (eds), *Comparative History of Urban Origins*, p. 439.

3. T. R. Slater, 'English medieval new towns with composite plans: evidence from the midlands', in T. R. Slater (ed.), *The Built Form of Western Cities* (Leicester, 1990), p. 70; Schofield and Vince, *Medieval Towns*, p. 35.

4. H. R. T. Summerson, *Medieval Carlisle*, 2 vols. (Kendal, 1993), p. 177.

5. E.g. J. M. Bennett, 'Feminism and history', *Gender and History*, 1 (1989), pp. 251–72.

6. B. A. Windeatt (ed.), *The Book of Margery Kempe* (Harmondsworth, 1985).

7. M. Bailey, 'Demographic decline in late medieval England', *Economic History Review*, 49 (1996), pp. 1–19; P. J. P. Goldberg, *Women, Work and Life Cycle in a Medieval Economy: York* (Oxford, 1992), pp. 346–7.

8. M. Kowaleski, The history of urban families in medieval England', *Journal of Medieval History*, 45 (1988), p. 55.

9. Phythian-Adams, *Desolation of a City*, pp. 227–8; S. Thrupp, *The Merchant Class of Medieval London* (Michigan, 1968), p. 204.

10. Phythian-Adams, *Desolation of a City*, pp. 92, 203.

11. *Ibid.*, p. 208; Carlin, *Medieval Southwark*, p. 138.

12. *Calendar of Patent Rolls Preserved in the Public Record Office. Henry VI*, 6 vols (London, 1901–10), vol. IV, 1436–41, p. 483.

13. Rosser, *Medieval Westminster*, pp. 193–4.

14. D. Keene, 'House, home and household at the heart of the city of London 1227–1638', paper given to the conference 'Houses and Households in Towns 100–1600', Birmingham, 1994.

15. Rosser, *Medieval Westminster*, p. 125.

16. Bonney, *Lordship and the Urban Community*, p. 165.

17. B. Harvey, *Living and Dying in England 1100–1530* (Oxford, 1993), p. 23.

18. Phythian-Adams, *Desolation of a City*, p. 132.

19. Miller and Hatcher, *Medieval England: Towns, Commerce and Crafts*, p. 336.

20. J. F. Pound, *Tudor and Stuart Norwich* (Chichester, 1988), p. 33.

21. Borthwick Institute, York, Dean and Chapter Original wills and inventories.

22. Kowaleski, *Local Markets and Regional Trade*, p. 126.

23. Pound, *Tudor and Stuart Norwich*, p. 32.

24. Gemmill and Mayhew, *Changing Values*, p. 379.

25. R. B. Dobson, 'Craft guilds and the city', in A. E. Knight (ed.), *The Stage as Mirror: Civic Theatre in Late Medieval Europe* (Cambridge, 1997), p. 105.

26. Thrupp, *Merchant Class*, p. 140.

27. Dyer, *Standards of Living in the Later Middle Ages* (Cambridge, 1989), p. 193.

28. Kowaleski, *Local Markets and Regional Trade*, p. 112.

29. Ewan, *Townlife in Fourteenth Century Scotland*, p. 121.

30. Nightingale, *Medieval Mercantile Community*, pp. 469, 529.

31. McNiocaill, 'Socio-economic problems', p. 14.

32. E. Miller, 'Rulers of thirteenth century towns: the cases of York and Newcastle upon Tyne', in Coss and Lloyd (eds) *Thirteenth Century England I*, p. 131.

33. R. Horrox, 'The urban gentry in the fifteenth century', in J. A. F. Thomson, *Towns and Townspeople in the Fifteenth Century* (Gloucester, 1988), p. 36.

34. J. Bossy, *Christianity in the West 1400–1700* (Oxford, 1985), p. 30.

152     Notes and References

35. B. A. Kumin, *The Shaping of a Community: The Rise and Reformation of the English Parish c.1400–1560* (Aldershot, 1996), p. 17.
36. Griffiths, *Boroughs of Mediaeval Wales*, p. 20.
37. I. Cowan, 'The emergence of the urban parish', in Lynch, Spearman and Stell (eds), *Scottish Medieval Town*, p. 93.
38. Kumin, *Shaping of a Community*, pp. 4–5.
39. Lydon, *Ireland in the Later Middle Ages*, p. 23.
40. R. N. Swanson, *Catholic England: Faith, Religion and Observance before the Reformation* (Manchester, 1993), p. 261.
41. E. Duffy, 'The parish, piety and patronage in late medieval East Anglia', in K. L. French (ed.), *The Parish in English Life* (Manchester, 1997), p. 133.
42. I. Cowan, 'Church and society', in J. M. Brown, *Scottish Society in the Fifteenth Century* (Arnold, 1977), p. 117.
43. Rosser, *Medieval Westminster*, pp. 269–71.
44. Duffy, 'Parish, piety and patronage', p. 141.
45. J. A. Ford, 'Marginality and the assimilation of foreigns in the lay parish community', in French, *Parish in English Life*, p. 210.
46. Carlin, *Medieval Southwark*, p. 90.
47. R. B. Dobson, 'Citizens and chantries in late medieval York', in D. Abulafia, M. Franklin and M. Rubin (eds), *Church and City 1000–1500* (Cambridge, 1992), pp. 324–5.
48. D. MacKay, 'Parish life in Scotland 1500–1560', in D. M. Roberts (ed.), *Essays on the Scottish Reformation* (Glasgow, 1962), p. 92.
49. G. Stell, 'Urban buildings', in Lynch, Spearman and Stell, *Scottish Medieval Town*, p. 68.
50. Kumin, *Shaping of a Community*, p. 77.
51. G. Rosser, 'Communities of parish and guild', in S. Wright (ed.), *Parish Church and People* (London, 1988), pp. 29–55.
52. M. Sellers (ed.), *York Memorandum Book*, vol. II (Surtees Society, 125, 1914), pp. 278–9.
53. McKay, 'Parish life in Scotland 1500–1560', p. 89.
54. J. Polsue, *Lake's Parochial History of the County of Cornwall*, vol. III (Truro, 1870, repr. Wakefield, 1974), p. 75.
55. B. O'Sullivan, 'The Dominicans in medieval Dublin', in H. Clarke (ed.), *Medieval Dublin: the Living City* (Dublin, 1990), p. 89.
56. A. F. Johnston and M. Rogerson (eds), *Records of Early English Drama: York*, vol. 2 (Manchester, 1979), p. 732; A. J. Mill, 'The Perth Hammermen's play, *Scottish Historical Review*, 49 (1970), pp. 152–3.
57. R. B. Dobson, 'Craft guilds and the city', in A. G. Knight (ed.), *The Stage as Mirror: Civic Theatre in Late Medieval Europe* (Cambridge, 1997), pp. 101, 104.
58. Hilton, *English and French Towns*, pp. 124–5.
59. N. Orme and M. Webster, *The English Hospital 1070–1570* (New Haven, 1995), p. 58.
60. Cowan, 'Church and society', p. 132.
61. Harvey, *Living and Dying*, pp. 23–4, 33; M. Rubin, *Charity and Community in Medieval Cambridge* (Cambridge, 1987), pp. 294–5.
62. Quoted in C. Rawcliffe, *The Hospitals of Medieval Norwich* (Norwich, 1995), p. 156.

63. M. Murphy, 'Pro anima bequests in medieval Dublin', in W. J. Sheils and D. Wood (eds), *The Church and Wealth. Studies in Church History vol. 24* (Oxford, 1987), p. 122.
64. C. M. Barron, 'Education in London', in Blair and Golding (eds), *Cloister and the World*, p. 278.
65. J. McQueen, 'The literature of fifteenth century Scotland', in J. M. Brown, *Scottish Society in the Fifteenth Century* (London, 1977), p. 204.
66. J. Moran, *The Growth of English Schooling 1340–1548* (Princeton, 1985), p. 163.
67. E. G. Duff, *The English Provincial Printers, Stationers and Bookbinders to 1557* (Cambridge, 1912), p. 34.
68. See above, p. 62.
69. P. Brand, *The Origins of the English Legal Profession* (Oxford, 1992), pp. 85–115.
70. R. N. Swanson, *Religion and Devotion in Europe c.1215–c.1515* (Cambridge, 1995), p. 244.
71. S. McSheffrey, *Gender and Heresy: Women and Men in Lollard Communities 1420–1530* (Philadelphia, 1995), pp. 60, 138.

## Conclusion

1. G. Sjoberg, *The Pre-Industrial City* (New York, 1960).
2. *The Chronicle of Lanercost, 1272–1346* (Glasgow, 1913), p. 156.

# SELECT BIBLIOGRAPHY

This bibliography is not comprehensive, and does not include all the works cited in the notes. It is intended to provide suggestions for the next stage of an inquiry into British medieval towns. It includes the works that I have most often referred to, together with some of the most useful essay collections and significant articles on the subject. The forthcoming *Cambridge Urban History of Britain Vol. I*, edited by D. Palliser, will be an essential reference work for English, Scottish and Welsh towns.

Bailey, M., 'A tale of two towns: Buntingford and Standon in the later middle ages', *Journal of Medieval History*, 19 (1993), pp. 351–71.

Bailey, M., 'Demographic decline in late medieval England', *Economic History Review*, 49 (1996), pp. 1–19.

Barron, C. M. and Sutton, A. F. (eds), *Medieval London Widows 1300–1500* (London, 1994).

Beresford, M. W., *New Towns of the Middle Ages: Town Plantation in England, Wales and Gascony* (London, 1967).

Bonney, M. *Lordship and the Urban Community: Durham and its Overlords 1250–1540* (Cambridge, 1990).

Britnell, R. H., 'The proliferation of markets in England, 1200–1349', *Economic History Review*, 2nd ser., 34 (1981), pp. 209–21.

Britnell, R. H., *Growth and Decline in Colchester 1300–1525* (Cambridge, 1986).

Britnell, R. H., *The Commercialisation of English Society 100–1500* (Cambridge, 1993).

Britnell, R. H., and Campbell, B. M. S. (eds), *A Commercialising Economy: England 1086–c1300* (Manchester, 1995).

Britnell, R. H. and Hatcher, J. (eds), *Progress and Problems in Medieval England* (Cambridge, 1996).

Brooke, C. N. L. and Keir, G., *London 800–1216: the Shaping of a City* (London, 1975).

Carlin, M., *Medieval Southwark* (London, 1996).

Carus-Wilson, E. M., *Medieval Merchant Venturers*, 2nd edn (London, 1967).

Clarke, H. (ed.), *Medieval Dublin*, 2 vols (Dublin, 1990).

Clarke, H. and Ambrosiani, B., *Towns in the Viking Age* (Leicester, 1991).

Clarke, H. B. and Simms, A. (eds), *The Comparative History of Urban Origins in Non-Roman Europe*, 2 vols (British Archaeological Reports International Ser., 255, 1985).

Cosgrove, A. (ed.), *A New History of Ireland. II. Medieval Ireland 1169–1534* (Oxford, 1987).

Davies, R. R., *Conquest, Coexistence and Change: Wales 1063–1415* (Oxford, 1987).

Dobson, R. B., 'Admissions to the freedom of the city of York in the later middle ages', *Economic History Review*, 2nd ser., 26 (1973), pp. 1–22.

Dobson, R. B., 'Citizens and chantries in late medieval York', in D. Abulafia, M. Franklin and M. Rubin (eds), *Church and City 1000–1500* (Cambridge, 1992).

Duncan, A. A. M., *Scotland, the Making of the Kingdom* (Edinburgh, 1975).

Dyer, A., *Decline and Growth in English Towns 1400–1640* (Cambridge, 1991).

Dyer, C., *Standards of Living in the Later Middle Ages* (Cambridge, 1989).

Dyer, C., 'Market towns and the countryside in late medieval England', *Canadian Journal of History*, 31 (1996), pp. 17–35.

Dyer, C., 'Medieval Stratford: a successful small town', in R. Bearman (ed.), *The History of an English Borough, Stratford-upon-Avon 1196–1996* (Stroud, 1997).

Ewan, E., *Townlife in Fourteenth Century Scotland* (Edinburgh, 1990).

Gemmill, E. and Mayhew, N., *Changing Values in Medieval Scotland: a Study of Prices, Money, Weights and Measures* (Cambridge, 1995).

Goldberg, P. J. P., *Women, Work and Life-cycle in a Medieval Economy: York* (Oxford, 1992).

Griffiths, P. A., *Boroughs of Mediaeval Wales* (Cardiff, 1978).

Gross, C., *The Gild Merchant*, 2 vols (Oxford, 1890).

Harding, A., *The Law Courts of Medieval England* (London, 1973).

Hilton, R. H., *Class Conflict and the Crisis of Feudalism* (London, 1985).

Hilton, R. H., *English and French Towns in Feudal Society: a Comparative Study* (Cambridge, 1992).

Holt, R. and Rosser, G. (eds), *The Medieval Town: a Reader in English Urban History 1200–1540* (London, 1990).

Jack, R. I., 'The cloth industry in medieval Wales', *Welsh History Review*, 10 (1981), pp. 443–60.

Kowaleski, M., *Local Markets and Regional Trade in Medieval Exeter* (Cambridge, 1995).

Kumin, B. A., *The Shaping of a Community: the Rise and Reformation of the English Parish c.1400–1560* (Aldershot, 1996).

Lydon, J., *Ireland in the Later Middle Ages* (Dublin, 1972).

Lynch, M. (ed.), *The Early Modern Town in Scotland* (London, 1986).

Lynch, M., Spearman, M. and Stell, G. (eds), *The Scottish Medieval Town* (Edinburgh, 1988).

McNeill, P. G. B. and MacQueen, H. L. (eds), *Atlas of Scottish History to 1707* (Edinburgh, 1996).

MacNiocaill, G., 'Socio-economic problems of the late medieval Irish town', in D. Harkness and M. O'Dowd (eds), *The Town in Ireland* (Belfast, 1981).

Masschaele, J., *Peasants, Merchants and Markets: Inland Trade in Medieval England 1150–1350* (London, 1996).

Miller, E., 'Rulers of thirteenth century towns: the cases of York and Newcastle upon Tyne', in P. R. Coss and S. D. Lloyd (eds), *Thirteenth Century England I* (Woodbridge, 1986).

Miller, E. and Hatcher, J., *Medieval England: Towns, Commerce and Crafts 1086–1348* (London, 1995).

Nightingale, P., 'Capitalists, crafts and constitutional change in late fourteenth century London', *Past and Present*, 124 (1989), pp. 3–35.

O'Brien, A. F., 'The royal boroughs, seaport towns and royal revenue in medieval Ireland', *Journal of the Royal Society of Antiquaries of Ireland*, 118 (1988), pp. 13–26.

Phythian-Adams, C., *Desolation of a City: Coventry and the Urban Crisis of the Later Middle Ages* (Cambridge, 1979).

Platt, C., *Medieval Southampton* (London, 1973).

Pound, J. P., *Tudor and Stuart Norwich* (Chichester, 1988).

Reynolds, S., *An Introduction to the History of English Medieval Towns* (Oxford, 1977).

Rigby, S. R., *English Society in the Later Middle Ages* (Macmillan, 1995).

Rosser, G., *Medieval Westminster, 1200–1540* (Oxford, 1989).

Rosser, G., 'Crafts, guilds and the negotiation of work in the medieval town', *Past and Present*, 154 (1997), pp. 3–31.

Schofield, J. and Vince, A., *Medieval Towns* (Leicester, 1994).

Slater, T. R. (ed.), *Urban Decline 100–1600* (forthcoming).

Slater, T. R. and G. Rosser (eds), *The Church in the Medieval Town* (Aldershot, 1998).

Soulsby, I, *The Towns of Medieval Wales* (Chichester, 1983).

Swanson, H. C., *Medieval Artisans: an Urban Class in Late Medieval England* (Oxford, 1989).

Tait, J., *The Medieval English Borough* (Manchester, 1936).

Thomas, A., *The Walled Towns of Ireland*, 2 vols (Dublin, 1992).

Thomson, J. A. F. (ed.), *Towns and Townspeople in the Fifteenth Century* (Gloucester, 1988).

Thrupp, S. L., *The Merchant Class of Medieval London* (Michigan, 1962).

Unwin, G., *The Gilds and Companies of London* (London, 1908).

Williams, G. A., *Medieval London: from Commune to Capital* (London, 1963).

# INDEX